UNIVERSITY OF THE NATIONS

UNIVERSITY
OF THE NATIONS

The Story of the Gregorian University
with Its Associated Institutes,
the Biblical and Oriental 1551–1962

by
Philip Caraman, S.J.

PAULIST PRESS
New York/Ramsey

The photograph of St. Ignatius is reprinted with
permission from Rahner/Loose, **Ignatius von Loyola,**
© *Verlag Herder Freiburg.*

The photograph of Pope Pius VII is used by permission
of The Keeper of the Queen's Pictures.
Copyright reserved.

Copyright © 1981
Philip Caraman, S.J.

Library of Congress Catalog Card Number: 80–84513

ISBN: 0–8091–2355–X

Published by Paulist Press
545 Island Road, Ramsey, N.J. 07446

Printed and bound in the United States of America

Introduction

Forty years ago at the university I was told, "Never try to write contemporary history. It can't be done." In this book I have kept this rule and with one exception I have not written about the living. For the rest I believe I have told a true story. I must admit that some of those who played a part in it have attracted me more than others, both popes and professors. As far as possible I have got away from the old type of self-laudatory literature of which the Society of Jesus produced so much on the occasion of its first centenary and has no appeal today, although its store of books contains some rich seams of information that cannot be found elsewhere. There are literally hundreds of men who spent many years of their life walking the corridors of the Roman College and mounting its rostrums who are not even mentioned: they were the journeymen of the professorial staff without whom the college could never have functioned. This does not mean to say that I have left out many figures of interest, but to keep the book within reasonable dimensions I have been forced to discard much material. Anyone attempting a full history of the Gregorian University would be obliged to spend several years in its archives before going on to explore the papers in at least half a dozen equally extensive Roman libraries.

This is unashamedly popular history, but popular history is mainly a matter of presentation and is not history at all unless it is based on reading and research. The bibliography at the end of this book is an honest one and faithfully gives the extent of my reading. It is not a bibliography of the university which would occupy several books the size of this.

My first intention was to divide the book into two more or less equal parts, the first taking the history of the Gregorian down to 1909 and the second dealing with the university together with its associated institutes, the Biblicum and Orientale. In the course of writing I rejected this plan because it would have upset the balance of the book and have involved a great deal of technical material that I was unqualified to handle and which, in any case, could scarcely have held the attention of a nonspecialist reader. Throughout I have tried to set the story against the background of contemporary events in Rome and Europe.

It was my good fortune many years ago to belong to a small group of students who met every week in the rooms of Sir Maurie Powicke, the Regius Professor of History at Oxford, who would talk about long forgotten bishops, kings and statesmen as though he had just come from entertaining them in the hall of his college. All that I learned then about the thirteenth century I have now forgotten, but one lesson I took away with me, namely, that there need never be an excuse for making history dull. I can only hope that the reader will discover in this book something of the fascination the subject had for me in writing it.

I must record my thanks to the Rector of the Gregorian University, Fr. Carlo Martini, now Archbishop of Milan, and to Frs. Maurice Gilbert and Eduard Huber, Rectors of the Biblical and Oriental Institutes, for their help and hospitality while I was preparing to write this book. The scientific sections owe much to Fr. Daniel O'Connell, formerly Director of the Vatican Observatory. Fr. Francis Courtney steered me through the quagmire of the *De Auxiliis* controversy, Fr. Robert Butterworth called my attention to passages in Newman's Correspondence, Fr. Joseph Barrett gave me the title I needed but could not find myself, and Fr. Henry Pfeiffer and Fr. Edmond Lamalle took many of the photographs for the illustrations. Very generously

UNIVERSITY OF NATIONS

Dr. Oskar Garstein of Oslo allowed me to read the proofs of his second volume on the Counter-Reformation in Scandinavia and the typescript of the third volume. But the book owes most to Fr. John E. Blewett who watched patiently over it from its conception to its completion.

Philip Caraman
Rome, February 1980

1

On February 17, 1580 a party of three Jesuits arrived at the court of the great Mogul Akbar at Fatehpur Sikri, near Agra. Their leader was Rudolf Acquaviva. The son of the Duke of Atri and on his mother's side related to Aloysius Gonzaga, he was a shy young Jesuit not yet thirty, absent-minded to the point of constantly forgetting where he had left his spectacles and books, and with the sometimes disconcerting habit of humming under his breath little songs composed by himself in honor of the Blessed Virgin. In a gown tattered and threadbare after a journey begun exactly three months earlier at Goa, he was ushered into the presence of the emperor, a reputed despot, the "Terror of India," whose kingdom included all northern Hindustan and stretched as far south as the central plains of Deccan. At the same time he was an intellectual, anxious to examine every system of religious belief found in his dominions. For the purpose of debates between Christians, Brahmins, Jains and Sunni Moslems he built and adorned a splendid conference hall, still to be seen, in his palace at Fatehpur, where he presided over religious and philosophical discussions. He was a freethinker and his aim was to find an ecumenical formula that would unite the divers creeds and religious customs of his people. In this way he hoped to build a more solid foundation for his authority. As part of this plan he had invited Acquaviva and his companions to his court.

Rudolf Acquaviva belonged to the second generation of students who had done their course of humanities at a school established by Ignatius Loyola in Rome in the year 1551; he was also the first of many alumni to distinguish themselves in the field of missionary enterprise.

The Roman College, as St. Ignatius called it, began in a rented house, number fourteen via Capitolina, on the lower northern slope of that hill, where today the via d'Aracoeli intersects the via Margana, an area still rural at the time and lying on the outskirts of the city close to the Roman forum. Its first rector was a Frenchman, Jean Pelletier, whose staff was drawn from the Jesuit residence adjoining the Church of Madonna della Strada. A donation from Francis Borgia, formerly Duke of Gandia and now a Jesuit, made it possible for Ignatius to pay the rent of the house and the pension of the students.*

It was the genius of St. Ignatius to see with compelling clarity the needs of his time and to provide for them from exiguous resources of men and money without for a moment losing faith in his first vision. From the day in Rome in 1548 when he first discussed the project with Fr. Diego Laynez, one of his early companions, Ignatius had in mind a model that would provide a four year course in humanities to be followed by seven years devoted to philosophy and theology. The plan conformed roughly to the educational system of the day, but Ignatius grafted on to it an innovation that was to make it a unique establishment in Europe. From the beginning he saw it as a university at the service of the Holy See in the center of the Catholic world with a staff of professors drawn from whatever country the most proficient in their subjects could be found.

The first scholastic year opened on February 23, 1551 with sixty scholars under fifteen teachers in five classes of grammar

---

*St. Francis Borgia made his solemn profession in Spain on August 26, 1550 and then set out for Rome, ostensibly to gain the jubilee indulgence, but in reality to arrange with St. Ignatius for his official entry into the Society. He was in Rome until February 4, 1551, the year the Roman College was founded.

and litterae humaniores. Hebrew was added to the syllabus in the following September. The rules drawn up for the rector make it clear that the college, far from being restricted to Jesuits, was open to all comers; in fact, as late as 1553 the number of Jesuits was only eleven. It was expected that at the end of their studies most of the students would return home thoroughly well educated, sound in morals and firm in their loyalty to the Holy See. It was with this in mind that Ignatius proscribed the reading of Ovid and Terence and ordered the works of Savonarola to be removed from the library and burned. He had nothing against the friar's teaching; in fact, he admired the quality of *Il Trionfo della Croce,* but disapproved of his strong anti-papal bias. As Ignatius explained to his secretary, "in temper Savonarola was a rebel against the Holy See and could not therefore be approved, although he had many good things to say."

It was a rule that all scholars had to attend daily Mass: they were to follow the priest devoutly, not squatting on the floor of the chapel or lolling against the walls, but kneeling or standing at the appropriate times. They were not allowed to walk out in the city at carnival times. When corporal punishment was necessary, it was to be administered by a layman. This was a firm principle laid down by St. Ignatius for all his schools with the exception of Gubbio where it was in the hands of senior students; but his experiment was later abandoned when scholars expecting punishment turned up armed, ready to exact vengeance on those who had chastised them.

In the autumn of 1553, just two years after the college had opened, a course of higher studies was inaugurated. This was the germ of the Gregorian University. For this purpose Ignatius summoned from Sicily Fr. Jerome Nadal who had master-minded Jesuit educational work in Messina, Portugal and Spain, a man with a great talent, as Ignatius described him in a letter to John III of Portugal. The first theological lecture was given on October 28, the feast of Sts. Simon and Jude, and at the same time courses were started in logic, ethics and physics. Looking ahead still further Ignatius intended to provide eventually another two years' study for those who wished to go on for doctorates in philosophy and theology.

It was the founder's hope that the Roman College would attract a large enrollment. From his letters it is clear that he wished to establish a model that would induce bishops to make similar foundations in their own dioceses for which the Roman College would provide highly trained professors.

While he never lost sight of his goal, Ignatius was continually harassed by lack of funds. Francis Borgia's gift of 800 scudi, which had made the foundation possible, was soon exhausted; promises of further gifts from his relatives were not honored. Pope Julius III, who did not hesitate to make use of Jesuit theologians at the Council of Trent, gave his blessing to Ignatius' project but died in 1555 without donating the funds he had promised. More than once it looked as if the college would have to close. Polanco, Ignatius' secretary, wrote a flurry of letters to Spain, Sicily and Naples begging for help: if the friends of the Jesuits were unable to send money, then gifts in kind—wine, cereals, clothing—were all welcome. Academic displays also formed part of Ignatius' means of attracting attention to his foundation. The first was held in May 1552 in the Church of Sant' Eustachio, and thereafter they became a regular feature of the scholastic programme. In the early years the display took the form of a dialogue or debate, or even a rudimentary drama, in which some incident of remote or recent history was discussed or portrayed. The argument usually lasted about two hours. It was the beginning of Jesuit drama for which the college was shortly to become famous. The first written rules, some ten years later, dealt with the performance of "dialogues, comedies and tragedies," which were to be given once a year at the opening of studies and were to be edifying and not deal with mythical subjects.

Ignatius also set great store by both the formal and the regular weekly disputations held in the schoolrooms: they soon shaped the style and methods adopted by generations of students in theological debates throughout Europe as well as in Asia. Sometimes they became tests of endurance, memory and fast thinking. Rudolph Acquaviva, once engaged in controversy with the mullahs of Akbar's court, quickly forgot his reticence. While his opponents had only a secondhand and sketchy knowledge of the Christian faith, for they were forbidden by Muslim law to study it, Acquaviva had come armed with a Portuguese translation of the Koran in which he had scored in the margin passages to reinforce his argument. However, his training at the Roman College had not prepared him for the test which Akbar cunningly proposed for the settlement of the controversy, namely, that a pit should be dug and filled with a fire so that a mullah holding the Koran and the Jesuit holding a Bible could in turn cast themselves into it to see whom God would protect.

In Rome while academic exercises fostered good will among friends, they attracted few benefactions. Soon after the foundation of the Roman College Ignatius faced even more acute financial problems over another house which, in spite of forecasts of failure, he had founded only eighteen months after the Roman College. The Germanicum was conceived not as an academy or gymnasium but as a hall of residence on the model of the colleges of the University of Paris where Ignatius and his first companions had themselves studied. It was formally established by a bull of Julius III, *Dum sollicita,* dated August 31, 1552.

From the start it catered exclusively to more mature students going on for the priesthood. As with the Roman College its first home was a rented house, near Sant' Andrea della Valle, and although some tuition was given there, the scholars attended lectures at the Roman College. But Ignatius' vision was not restricted to Germany. In an exchange of letters with Cardinal Pole, Archbishop of Canterbury (in 1550 Pole had lost the papal election by one vote to Julius III owing to the Roman prejudice against foreigners), Ignatius considered the foundation of a similar college for England. His scheme for a Hungarian College came nearer realization, but in the end provision for Hungarians was found with the Germans. The German-Hungarian College, as it then came to be called, was the first of scores of institutions that were to send students to the Roman College during the next four centuries.

Credit for its establishment was in part due to Cardinal Morone, the papal nuncio in Germany. He and Ignatius had discussed a foundation of the kind as a means of rebuilding the Church in Germany: they agreed that in Rome young Germans would be given the best scholastic formation the Church offered and would return to their dioceses with a strong attachment to the papacy to fill the principal benefices in their country. Julius III accepted the idea with enthusiasm and placed the foundation under Jesuit government. From its first years it took in students from Bohemia, Poland, Hungary, England and the Scandinavian countries.

But Ignatius' immediate problem was to find the right type of candidates for the German College. Twelve months after its foundation he wrote to Peter Canisius in Vienna and to the Jesuit superiors in Ingolstad and Louvain; he pressed them to send to Rome youths between the ages of sixteen and twenty-two or even older, selected for their ability, good manners, sound health and capacity to undertake an exacting course of studies. Canisius, though sick, was the first to reply. He promptly pointed to the flaws he saw in Ignatius' plans: "It is extremely difficult," he wrote, "to persuade the people of Austria to send their sons to Rome, for the conditions of entrance are the kind no northerners will tolerate, especially the one that requires students to bind themselves to the service of the Pope!" Canisius referred also to the rumors he had heard that the college had so far not proved a success and was in danger of shutting down. This provoked a sharp retort from Ignatius: the college, he insisted, was doing well, the students had two days' holiday each week in the country and greater progress was possible in Rome in one year than in two elsewhere. Ignatius' persistent optimism is seen also in a letter he wrote to Francis Xavier in the Far East in July 1553; although there were only twenty-nine students in the German College at the time of writing, he hoped soon for a hundred. Eighteen months later, in March 1555, in a letter to his close friend, Gerard Kalckbrenner, the Prior of the Carthusians at Cologne, he said that "the number was now fifty." The increase was due mainly to Peter Canisius who in April of the previous year had sent Ignatius twenty-four men from all parts of Austria and Germany at the sacrifice of more immediate needs at home.

It was Canisius' action that made possible the inauguration of the full course of higher studies at the Roman College. As though he knew he had only a short time left in which to work, Ignatius set about organizing the syllabus with a sense of immediate urgency. According to his directive, Aquinas rather than Augustine, Peter Lombard or Duns Scotus was to form the basis for the course of theology. This was by no means an obvious decision and was considered a surprising innovation at the time. The clear style of the *Summa* and its pedagogical excellence appealed to Ignatius, who believed it to be the most faithful summary of Christian thought available. At the same time he set about looking for a companion textbook of scholastic theology more suited to his time. At first he enlisted for the task Diego Laynez who began work on a compendium of theology in 1553, but after six or seven weeks had to abandon the task for lack of time. Salmeron was then approached. Like Laynez, he was both an early companion of Ignatius and a papal theologian at Trent. Called to Rome at Easter 1554, he could stay there less than three weeks because the Viceroy of Naples, where he was working, insisted on his immediate return.

However, Ignatius went ahead with the establishment of a printing press at the Roman College. If it could not be used to provide a new *Summa,* it could turn out for poorer students a much needed supply of cheap texts as well as classical ones of Roman authors expurgated of their less delicate passages. He had hoped first for the gift of a press in the possession of Duke Cosimo de' Medici, but was disappointed. He then wrote to the Jesuits in Venice, famous throughout Europe for its excellent typefaces, asking them to search for a set of type at bargain price. Two months before Ignatius' death on July 31, 1556, it arrived in Rome but the letters were found to be too small for easy reading and only in the following autumn was a press found and purchased in Rome. The first book printed after its installation was the *Epigrams of Martial,* edited by the Latin master at the college, Fr. André des Freux.

Ignatius had lived to see what he considered his most important work well-established though far from financially secure. Paul IV, Julius' successor, had granted both the German and Roman Colleges a small subsidy in 1555 but had discontinued it after a year. Days of extreme poverty followed. Many believed both places were doomed to closure, but not Ignatius. One of his last acts was to send Jerome Nadal, whom he greatly needed in Rome, on a desperate begging mission to Spain; another was to summon to Rome Fr. James Ledesma, a theologian with a tidy and practical turn of mind, who had done the deviling for Laynez at Trent. Ledesma did more than fill one of the two chairs of scholastic theology, he produced the up-to-date *Summa* Ignatius had wanted so much; he called it simply *Christian Doctrine*. It was translated into ten languages, including English* and made his name famous from Lithuania to the savage tribes of Canada. What was equally important, he formulated a number of pedagogical principles, which were incorporated into the famous Jesuit educational charter, the *Ratio Studiorum,* which was published in 1575, some years after his death.

For five years Ignatius had nursed the Roman College as the pivot of the entire educational system of his newly formed Society; the most suitable educational methods were to be tested there, its curricula used in other colleges, and the textbooks printed at its press dispatched all over Europe. He had planned also to set up books in Arabic for the conversion of the Muslim, his first apostolic dream which, along with a love of poverty, he shared with Francis of Assisi. Books were also to be printed for use in Ethiopia where his men were already at work. He had seen the premises in the via Capitolina become too confined and in November 1551 he had transferred the college to a building or rather to a collection of miserable tenements behind the Church of San Stefano del Cacco and close to his own residence. This move inspired him to discuss with his friend, Michelangelo, the project of a church which the old man, now eighty, had offered to build without charging a fee. It was only Ignatius' scruple against evicting some tenants on the proposed site that prevented the realization of the scheme.

Within those five years the college had achieved academic acclaim. Ignatius had hesitated to seek for it the title of university, in order not to appear to compete with the Sapienza, the

---

*The French translation was made by St. Jean de Brébeuf, the North American martyr.

UNIVERSITY OF NATIONS

Roman university founded orginally by Boniface VIII in 1303 and reconstituted by Leo X in 1513. However, by a *motu proprio* of January 17, 1556, the year of Ignatius' death, the college had received the right to grant doctorates in philosophy and theology and had been granted all the privileges enjoyed by the universities of Paris, Louvain, Salamanca and Alcalà.

2

A second change of location occurred a year following the death of Ignatius after the Roman College and the Jesuit residence attached to the Church of Santa Maria della Strada had been flooded on the night of September 14, in a great inundation of the Tiber. "Never in my life have I seen anything so extraordinary and terrifying," wrote Polanco. The Fathers spent the night in the upper rooms of their house, led in prayer by Diego Laynez who had succeeded Ignatius as head of the Society. New premises for the college were found at once in the Palazzo Salviati at the corner of the via Lata and the via della Strada, which twenty-seven years later were pulled down to make room for Gregory XIII's new spacious building. By the end of October the palazzo was furnished and ready for the opening of schools.

Laynez's problems were as pressing as Ignatius' had been. The German College, that accounted for the greatest number of non-resident students, was still in difficulties. Peter Canisius in Vienna was so convinced it was again on the brink of dissolution that he submitted plans to Rome for an alternative college on German soil. Laynez would have none of it. Not until eleven years later when Canisius, now an old man, was appointed papal

14

adviser on German affairs, was he fully convinced that he had been wrong. He then confessed that he found it difficult to advise the pope on appointments, "seeing that in this country there is scarcely a man to be found who willingly declares, or desires others to believe, that he is in any special grace with the pope." Canisius died at Freiburg in 1597 but not before he had seen the fulfillment of Ignatius' vision, for by the end of the century the bishops of Salzburg, Breslau, Augsburg, Trieste, Würzburg and Passau were all former students of the German College. "Our success," wrote the papal nuncio at that time, "is clearly due to the work of the young men educated in Rome; they have an enthusiasm for the Roman cause that the majority of the clergy lack."

Although in its first five years the Roman College had won limited acclaim, it was a long way from becoming the university of all nations that Ignatius had conceived.

It was not until 1562 that it began to take on a truly international character. In that year Cardinal Borromeo, not yet a priest, a nephew of the Milanese pope, Pius IV, visited the college in company with the Spanish ambassador. The students who were assembled to greet their guests were divided into seventeen national groups. Ten years later the cardinal, now Archbishop of Milan and the founder of a seminary in his diocese which he had placed under the direction of the Jesuits, came again and met a similar reception. On both occasions he remarked that at a time of national rivalries it was astonishing how many different nations could live harmoniously together in the same college under one roof. There were students there from Flanders, Sweden, Estonia, England and Albania as well as from the southern countries of Europe. The place was beginning to look like a replica of Europe, *mundi quasi compendium.* Polanco, Ignatius' old secretary, claimed that in the late sixties most students could preach fluently in two languages and could make themselves understood in four or five.

In 1564 the college gained a great increase in the number of students attending lectures when Pius IV placed the direction of the Roman seminary in the hands of the Jesuits. The move was inspired by the evident success of the German College and by the statutes of the English synod held by Cardinal Pole in 1556. Anxious to establish in Rome a seminary that could be made a pattern for all dioceses, the pope found himself faced with the problem of finding suitable professors. A commission of Cardinals appointed to examine the question suggested unanimously that, since the Jesuits had proved themselves competent in the Roman College, they should be entrusted with the seminary. The Roman clergy themselves strongly opposed the suggestion: they had come to distrust the Jesuits who had been given by the Cardinal Vicar of Rome the delicate task of examining ordinands and candidates for diocesan benefices. Pius IV, however, after some hesitation came down on the side of his cardinals.

The first seat of the seminary was the palazzo of the late Cardinal Pio da Carpi. On November 1, 1564 twenty Jesuits moved in under their rector, Giovanni Battista Perusio, the confessor of Philip Neri. At the start of the year the students numbered sixty-three. Hitherto the well-educated Roman clergy had been more canonists and men of letters than theologians. Now the new generation of students followed the full course of philosophy and theology at the Roman College.

Laynez, successor of Ignatius as General of the Order, knew the mind of Ignatius better than anyone. Hence, he was convinced that the college, given the best available staff of professors, would continue to draw students from all quarters. Already Ledesma, as a teacher, was beginning to attract attention beyond Rome. Soon he was joined in the second chair of theology by another Spaniard, Juan Mariana, a brilliant but erratic theologian only twenty-three at the time of his appointment. In the chair of philosophy was a Portuguese, Manoel da Saa, who had once been Francis Borgia's tutor. After recovering from a breakdown in health in 1559 he returned to fill the chair of exegesis. His reputation as a scholar led to his appointment to the commission set up for the revision of the vulgate of St. Jerome. From his published works it can been seen that he had a clear and masterly way of exposing the literal meaning of the Scriptures.

Da Saa and Ledesma were not the only professors of the

St. Ignatius Loyola (1491–1556)

The Roman College: Gregory XIII's building

St. Peter Canisius (1521–1597)

Gregory XIII (1502–1585)

Fr. Francesco Suarez (1548–1617)

Fr. Gabriel Vasquez (1549–1604)

Roman College to attain fame beyond its walls. Francesco de Toledo, a native of Córdoba, was summoned to Rome by Francis Borgia in 1559. While teaching first philosophy and then theology he held simultaneously the post of preacher to the papal court for twenty-four years. He was sent by the Holy See on several missions, including one to Paris where he reconciled Henry IV to the Catholic Church. In the Roman College he faithfully interpreted St. Thomas as Ignatius had laid down and published four volumes of commentaries on his works which made the college known in the schools of northern Europe. He was the first member of the college and the first Jesuit to be made a cardinal.

Gian Battista Eliano, a man of very different background, was also used on papal missions. He was a Jew from Venice who had been received into the Church by the Jesuits there. In November 1561 he interrupted his teaching to visit, on behalf of the pope, the Coptic Patriarch of Alexandria who was falsely reported to be seeking reunion with Rome.

With another Jesuit, he rode across the sands on a camel in search of the ancient patriarch of eighty-five, who was in the habit of retiring to a remote hermitage in the desert of St. Anthony. He had more success on a later mission to the Maronites of Syria. It was under his direction that the college press produced an Arabic translation of the canons and decrees of Trent, and also an Arabic New Testamant for the use of Christians in the Near and Middle East. But it was in the field of mathematics that the college first attained wide fame in Catholic countries and notoriety in the Protestant north.

Christopher Clavius, an alumnus of the college, joined the teaching staff in 1565 when he was a student in his third year of theology. For the next forty-seven years he held the chair of mathematics which formed part of the course of philosophy and included astronomy, geography and physics. In a memorandum he drew up on the teaching of his subject, he stressed the necessity of a sound understanding of it for a proper training in philosophy. "It would be helpful," he wrote, "if in individual conversations teachers were to encourage scholars to learn mathematics, impressing on them its necessity, and not doing the opposite. In this way there will be removed all that disagreement that is observed among us by externs when such opinions are heard in our schools." He insisted that mathematics had much to say on such matters as the division of the continuum, rainbows, sun and moon halos and other meteorological phenomena. "We could cite," he continues, "infinite instances from Aristotle, Plato and their great commentators, which are completely unintelligible without a fair knowledge of mathematics." Then writing from his experience which was, in fact, confined to Rome, he said he knew "many professors of philosophy who have made no end of mistakes, and most serious mistakes, and what is worse have published them, owing to their ignorance of mathematics."

Clavius won his case. He set the Roman College on a course of scientific study and research that was maintained until the end of the nineteenth century.

However, the greater part of Clavius' time outside the lecture room was devoted to the reform of the Julian calendar. As far back as the thirteenth century the English Franciscan, Roger Bacon, had pointed out its inadequacies and suggested its modernization. The Council of Trent took the matter up and in its last session referred it to the pope who formed a committee of which Clavius was the leading member. The final draft of its report, mainly his work, was presented to Pope Gregory XIII on September 14, 1580. According to the old Julian calendar the solar day was reckoned to be 11.14 seconds too long, so that one complete day was lost every one hundred and twenty-eight years. Clavius' calculations were so precise that an error of one day, on the new calendar, would occur only after the year 3333. When Gregory XIII's bull adopting the calendar was published early in 1582, October 5 of that year became October 15.

While most Catholic countries accepted the alteration at once, there was violent opposition from the Greeks who interpreted the change as another attempt at domination by Rome. Although Luther had insisted that no religious issue could be involved in a reform of the calendar, it was denounced in Protestant Germany as an example of interference with the divine arrangement of the universe. Riots broke out and in places the Catholic clergy were forcibly prevented from using the new calendar. But as the excitement died down, Clavius wrote his defense, or *Explicatio,* of the new calendar at the command of Clement VIII. He had the support of two leading astronomers of the day, Tycho Brahe, the Dane, and the German, Johann Kepler. In spite of this, it was not until the second half of the eighteenth century that the Protestant countries, Holland, Switzerland, Sweden and England accepted the change.

The reform had been inspired by Gregory XIII, Ugo Boncompagni, a Bolognese, who had succeeded to the papacy in 1572. The growing fame of Clavius and other professors had brought the Roman College to his attention: not only were they beginning to draw an annually increasing enrollment, but their success induced the pope to set about the reform of ecclesiastical education on Ignatius' model.

Gregory had been crowned only eight months when he gave a commission to Peter Canisius to visit the Catholic princes of Germany, Austria and Poland to get their views on the best way of strengthening Catholicism in the northern countries. The answer was unanimous: more educated priests and the endowment of the German College. To the report Canisius added his own pleadings when he came to Rome in the spring of 1573 for the election of a successor to Francis Borgia, who as the Jesuit General had died the previous October.

The first of Gregory's many initiatives was to set the German College on a firm financial basis after twenty years of precarious existence. On August 6, 1573, acting probably on the report of Canisius, he guaranteed the college an annual income of 10,000 ducats from the papal treasury, a sum reckoned sufficient for the support of a hundred students from Germany and the bordering nations. At the same time, through Cardinal Ptolomeo Gallio whose office corresponded roughly to that of the present day Secretary of State, he wrote to his nuncios in the northern countries ordering them to find suitable candidates. The next year Gregory followed his donation with the handsome gift of the Church and palace of Sant' Apollinare.

Through the registers of the college it is possible to trace the response to the pope's appeal in countries that had long lost contact with Rome. Between 1574 and 1578 nine Swedes, one

Dane, two Finns and another two described as Goths entered the German College, six of whom arrived on the same day, January 24, 1578 and another four on October 2. Their recruitment was the work of a Jesuit, Antonio Possevino, Vicar Apostolic of the northern countries that had no resident hierarchy. At a period when nations changed their religious allegiance with the faith of their sovereign, Gregory's hopes for the recovery of Sweden to the Catholic faith were not as vain as might now appear.

In 1574 John III of Sweden had declared his readiness to negotiate the return of his country to Catholicism, an astonishing *volte-face* for a son of Gustavus Vasa who had opted for Protestantism in order to finance his *parvenu* dynasty with the confiscated property of the Church. John's approach to Rome was due to his forceful Polish wife, Catherine Jagiellonika. With Gregory's approval Possevino concerted with the king a stratagem calculated to overcome the anti-Catholic prejudices of his people. Thus it happened that one day there appeared in Stockholm an unknown Protestant professor of theology, Lorenz Nicolai, who began a striking series of university lectures on Lutheranism. His instant success made it possible for the king to appoint him professor at the newly founded Protestant seminary in the city. The king urged the clergy to attend, and he himself with his court sat on the front benches of the auditorium. At the start, Nicolai exposed Luther's doctrine with such depth and precision that he won the excited admiration of his hearers; then suddenly, when he knew he had his audience with him, he began to adopt a critical tone. As the days passed his strictures became more radical and finally totally compelling. Nicolai, in fact, was a Norwegian Jesuit* in disguise. All seemed ready for the opening of negotiations with Rome in a sympathetic atmosphere when the queen died. With his second marriage to a Protestant lady, John's interest in Catholicism slowly evap-

---

*He came from the town of Larvik in Vestfold where a Norwegian Catholic family is today living on the property that once belonged to his family. His Norwegian name was Laurits Nielssen which was latinized as Laurentius Norvegus.

orated. But until the end of the decade and after, the flow of Swedish students to the German College continued. Later it became a sad trickle.

As with Sweden it was possible that England also would once more change her religion should Mary Queen of Scots or her son James or one of several Catholic claimants succeed to the throne on the death of Elizabeth. Already Cardinal Allen had prepared for this likely event (for Elizabeth had no obvious heir) by establishing at Douai in 1568 a house for English students who attended lectures at the university in the town. But he had neither the funds nor the facilities for the yearly increasing number of vocations. Turning toward Rome, and working through Dr. Owen Lewis, a legal official in the papal curia, Allen presented to Gregory the case for the foundation of an English College in the city. In 1576 students had already begun to arrive and to lodge in the old established English hospice for pilgrims. In May 1579 Gregory suppressed the hospice in the via Monserrato and another English hospice in Trastevere and gave their revenues and buildings to a Roman English seminary.

About the same time, the pope founded in the district of Trevi a college for the Maronites. This was the direct result of the mission of Father Eliano, the professor of Hebrew at the Roman College, to Syria. Owing to the advance of the Turks into the Adriatic and their control of the eastern Mediterranean, the Maronites had lost contact with the West. On his first journey Eliano had found that a number of dubious customs had infiltrated the Maronite church isolated as it was among Moslems. He reported to Rome and on his return to Syria in 1580 conducted a synod in the monastery at Quannobin, where everything was set right. Gregory was delighted, founded the college and put it under Jesuit direction. Another college for the Armenians met with failure. Gregory founded a third college, at the suggestion of Philip Neri, for young men converted from Judaism. A Greek College followed in 1577, which the pope again entrusted to the Jesuits; he gave it a handsome endowment including a residence in the via del Babuino, where the Greek liturgy was celebrated. Most of its scholars came from the

Venetian possessions in the Levant. Like the English and Germans they also attended lectures at the Roman Colleges.*

But it was the Roman College that benefited most from Gregory's munificence. His first action was to condone its debts; he then provided an endowment for the maintenance of two hundred students, and finally planned for it a magnificent new building, the work of Bartolomeo Ammanati, the architect of the Pitti palace in Florence. The site the pope chose was between the Church of Minerva and the Corso. Demolitions, begun in the summer of 1581, altered the appearance of the entire area. On January 11, 1582 the foundation stone was laid by Cardinal Guastavillani, with an inscription indicating that the college was to serve the education of the youth of all nations in the finest branches of knowledge. Coins struck on the occasion expressed the same idea—that it was to become a seminary for all Europe. On the outer wall of the building the inscription read: *"Gregory XIII—for religion and learning."*

The pope visited the site several times. As more and more money was needed for the construction, he provided it. Apart from a few disfigurements, the long simple façade stands today as it was then, the danger of monotony saved by a clever arrangement of windows that give life to the great mass of stonework. In contrast with the simplicity of the exterior is the elaborate cortile, spacious, dignified, unadorned, enclosed in a double arcade. It was the best Gregory could do for his favored college and the finest monument to his work for seminaries. While the new building was going up the college lost one of its most distinguished professors, Juan de Maldonato, who had taught there in 1563 for a short time and then been recalled to Rome by Gregory XIII in 1581 to work along with his fellow professor, Manoel da Saa, on a revision of the Septuagint. There is no description of his classes held in Rome but at the Jesuit College of Claremont in the precincts of the University of Paris not only students, but professors, bishops, and doctors of the

---

*Gregory also subsidized seminaries all over Italy, especially in Naples and Venice, as well as a seminary for Dalmatia and Illyria established at Loreto. In Milan he founded a Swiss college for priests serving the Catholic cantons of Switzerland.

Sorbonne came to his lectures in such crowds that he had to teach in the open. His commentaries on the Four Gospels were reckoned the best of their time and quickly found Protestant translators. Back in Rome he was visited by his close friend, Michel de Montaigne, who records in his *Journal de Voyage* the impression made on him by the Roman College. "It is marvellous," he wrote, "what a place this college holds in Christendom. I think there is no such other . . . C'est une pépinière de grands hommes en toute sorte de grandeur." Maldonato was only fifty when he died on the rostrum on January 5, 1583.

For more than thirty years the college had struggled to survive. Gregory had now secured its future and with justice was revered as its second founder. The new building was ready for the opening of the school year 1584. On the feast of Sts. Simon and Jude, October 28, the old pope, now eighty-two, still with luster in his blue eyes, and striking in appearance with the his long white beard and aquiline nose, was carried into the *salone* decorated with paintings of the colleges he had founded in Rome and elsewhere. Many cardinals were in his train. At the foot of his throne sat the students in the different habits of their colleges, the Roman seminarians in violet, the Germans in scarlet, the Greeks in their caftan and Venetian biretta, and some thirty young men from Capranica, who could claim pride of place, for their college had been founded ninety-five years before the Germanicum by two cardinal brothers whose name it bore. To an address of thanks in twenty-five languages the pope replied simply *"Soli Deo honor et gloria."* He then made a tour of the classrooms and in each received an elaborately composed paean of thanks from the scholars. He lived on only to March of the following year but in his last months he was still planning further colleges for the Irish in Rome, for the Albanians and Serbs at Lecce or Bari and was considering a seminary in Poland on the model of the German College.

3

Present at the solemn opening of the new college building was Francesco Suarez, a native of Granada, who had been summoned by Gregory XIII to teach in Rome and whose inaugural lecture the pope himself attended. In a comparatively short stay of five years (1580-85) Suarez did for the teaching of philosophy at the Roman College what Clavius had already achieved for the sciences. In the Preface to the complete edition of his *Mathematical Works* Clavius describes the confusion he found in the school of philosophy on his arrival in Rome and contrasted it with the uniformity of belief in mathematical truths: conflicting systems were taught side by side; in the same univeristy there were sometimes chairs for the teaching of Aquinas, Durandus, a Dominican of the next generation to Aquinas and a determined anti-Thomist, and Biel, a Nominalist, "the last of the scholastics" and the most popular of them all. Ignatius had opted for Aristotle in philosophy and Aquinas in theology but, as Clavius was quick to point out, the text of Aristotle was explained slavishly and without reference to the scientific developments that were already agitating the schools of Europe, a criticism borne out by notes of Robert Bellarmine made in his student days at the college. One entry reads: "Lectures on the second book of *De Anima* came to an end on Thursday evening, it being April 22 in the year of the Lord 1563, on which day the professor fell ill." The professor, Fr. Peter Parra, was back in his chair four days later, and continued to teach both morning and evening until his lectures on the single work of Aristotle totalled one hundred and twenty-eight. Clearly the time had come for a philosophical system which, preserving what was best in the traditional teaching, found a place for the new thought.

A vigorous thinker and only thirty-two at the time of his appointment, Suarez imposed his personality on his hearers both by his system and his style, setting forth old truths in a new context and discarding obsolete opinions or invalid arguments. At times he incurred bitter criticism, but it served only to give him the opportunity clearly to explain his method. He admitted that his approach was different from that of others; he did not teach through a copybook: "I have tried," he wrote once to the General of the Jesuits, "to leave this track. Hence my lectures offer some novelty, whether it be in the arrangement or in the manner of expression, or in the problems I raise which others do not, or in other matters. Thus while my teaching is not new, it becomes new in the manner of exposition and in its deviation from copybook routine."

Unfortunately, the Roman climate did not suit Suarez's health. After five years he returned to Spain but not before he had worked out, in the lecture halls of the new Roman College, the outline of his principal work, the *Disputationes Metaphysicae*, published twelve years later. The book created a storm in Europe. Although it contained over a thousand folio pages it went into twenty editions in the space of a few years, and the profits from it enabled the Jesuits to add a wing to their college in Salamanca as well as extend its library. The founders of modern philosophy used it as their textbook. Descartes carried it with him to Stockholm on his last journey there. Leibnitz, as a boy, found it in his father's library and read it like a novel. Schopenhauer treated it as a "true compendium of scholastic wisdom."

More than twenty years after leaving the Roman College Suarez, still in Spain, was working in cooperation with a former colleague on the staff of the Roman College, Robert Bellarmine, in the area of political philosophy where his influence was to be even more enduring. Like Clavius, Bellarmine, a Tuscan from Montepulciano, had won a reputation as a teacher before his ordination to the priesthood. In 1576 Gregory XIII called him from Louvain to Rome to fill the chair of controversy. The assignment was a difficult one for the chair, though established in 1561, had twice fallen vacant for the lack of an able occupant. At the same time it was clear that the course of scholastic theology by itself was insufficient training for religious debate.

As a student Bellarmine had concentrated on the partially neglected subjects of Church history, patristics and Scripture. He gave his first lecture on November 27, 1576. A fragment of it survives and shows the comprehensive clarity of his thought and positive approach to his subject. "We shall begin by treating of the Church," he said, "and in this disputation we shall have, first of all, to speak of Christ himself, who is the Church's head and ruler. Then we shall discuss that part of the Church which is laboring on earth under its visible head, the pope. Next, the Church suffering will claim our attention and finally that part of the Church which triumphs blessedly with Christ in heaven. At this point we shall have occasion to speak of the veneration and invocation of the saints, of relics, sacred images and similar matters; and after this of the communion of saints, under which heading the sacraments may be grouped. Each sacrament will have a whole treatise to itself . . . Last of all we shall deal with the tenth article of the creed under which come various debatable matters concerning grace, justification, free will and merit."

Bellarmine's lectures were later published in three volumes under the title *Disputationes de Controversiis Christianae Fidei,* a monumental work that brought order into the total chaos of controversy between Catholics and Protestants. The work was novel in its time for the scrupulous fairness with which he presented the position of his opponents; in tone and manner it had no resemblance to the current polemical writing. While pointing out the weakness of his adversaries, Bellarmine also made clear the strength of their position.

When the second tome appeared in 1588 the rector of the Jesuit house in Mainz wrote to Rome on September 28 that year to say that although "the Frankfurt (Book) Fair was not as grand as usual, every copy of Bellarmine's second volume was bought out immediately, and if the booksellers had had two thousand copies for disposal not one of them would have been left on their hands." Another Jesuit wrote from Louvain about the first volume that had appeared two years earlier: "I hear it is being studied everywhere, even by educated laymen and members of the parliament. The copies that came from Rome were gone the day they arrived."

The third volume was delayed twelve months by Bellarmine's appointment as rector of the Roman College in 1592.

Within a hundred years of publication, close to two hundred full-length replies to Bellarmine's work appeared in northern Europe, some running into three or four volumes. The authors represented almost every country and creed: Lutherans, Anabaptists, Jews, Zwinglians and Socinians; they ranged from uncontrolled abuse to reasoned argumentation. Among the first to reply was William Whitaker, a Cambridge Puritan from Burnley in Lancashire, an excellent scholar and an ardent exponent of orthodox Calvinism. His twenty or more works, written in Latin, had a wide circulation on the Continent and at least seven of them carried the name of Bellarmine on their title page. He had been awarded the Regius Professorship of theology largely on the strength of his thesis that "the Roman pontiff is the anti-Christ which the Scriptures have foretold will come." Bellarmine kept a print of an engraved portrait of Whitaker in his room. It helped him to enter the mind of his adversary. St. Francis de Sales, when a student in Padua University in 1588, was introduced to the first volume of the *Controversies.* Six years later he began his famous mission in the Calvinist region of Chablis. He often had to make his way across mountains and through snow and ice, and, although he reduced his baggage to a minimum, he wrote: "During five years in Chablis I preached with no other books than the Bible and those of the great Bellarmine."

Bellarmine, Suarez and Clavius gave a distinction to the Roman College that attracted the notice of academic Europe. Although Suarez's stay had been short, his successor, Gabriel

Vasquez, won hardly less renown. Brilliant and mercurial, he was called from Alcalá to fill the chair vacated by his compatriot. In every way he was the foil of his predecessor. Concise, witty and spontaneous, he was perhaps the most spellbinding lecturer the college had known. He did not have the profundity of Suarez, but he excelled him in the presentation of his subject; his Latin was epigrammatic and elegant, his mind sharp and his knowledge of the Councils and Augustine encyclopedic. This *Augustinus Redivivus,* as the students called him, defended Anselm's ontological argument for the existence of God, which had been rejected by Suarez, and maintained that the indwelling of the Holy Spirit consisted in the grace necessary for any good work. In fact, every exciting theological notion found its advocate in him. Free-lancing in his speculation, he reverted to the theory of Scotus on the Eucharist that the total "annihilation" of the bread was followed by the "adduction" of the body of Christ, thus removing the need for Thomas' theory of transubstantiation defended by Suarez. With his enthusiasm went a charming personality, genial, witty, vivacious. He relished his work and enjoyed the applause of his pupils. His lively controversies with his distinguished predecessor were compared to the exchanges between Jerome and Augustine. When his own *De Cultu Adorationis* was published Suarez detected in it fifteen propositions which he judged should be condemned. Vasquez replied with a list of thirty-two from Suarez's works which he maintained deserved similar treatment. But the influence of both teachers was enduring. More than a century after Vasquez's death Pope Benedict XIV, in a diocesan synod, referred to him as "the light of theologians."

More even than Vasquez, Robert Bellarmine impressed his personality on the students in his own unassuming manner. He was at the Roman College for a longer period and in different capacities, first as lecturer, then as spiritual director and finally as rector. After his name had become a household word in Europe, Protestant visitors to Rome would seek him out in his room so that on their return home they could boast that they had actually conversed with the most formidable champion of the papacy. In every case the encounter reversed their preconceptions. One honest account of such a visit survives naively written by a Protestant English traveler, Fynnes Moryson, who was in Rome in 1594, the year after the publication of the third volume of *Controversies*. Moryson admitted to an "obstinate purpose to see Bellarmine," but before he approached the Roman College he purchased a horse which he tethered at an inn outside the city center so that he could make a quick getaway to Siena if there was need to save his skin. He then boldly approached the gates and waited there for Bellarmine who, as the students told him, was out walking in the fields. Then, as Bellarmine returned, Moryson followed him up the staircase to his room. "Thus I came into Bellarmine's chamber," he narrates, "that I might see this man so famous for his learning and so great a champion of the pope who seemed not above forty years (he was actually fifty-two at the time) being lean of body and somewhat low of stature, with a little sharp beard upon his chin, of a brown color, and a countenance not very grave, and for his middle age wanting the authority of grey hairs."

Although Bellarmine received his visitor with great courtesy, he failed to put him wholly at his ease. As a measure of caution Moryson pretended he was a Frenchman on pilgrimage to Rome in order to fulfill a religious vow and to see the monuments. He then showered compliments on the rector who answered gently and gravely without swallowing the praise given him. Bellarmine assured him that he was welcome to come again whenever he chose. Moryson, having achieved his purpose, thanked the Jesuit, and after an exchange of courtesies made a quick exit "having nothing less in mind than to come again to him." There were cases, a contemporary on the staff states, when northern Protestants came to the Roman College together with an attorney to attest their visit to Bellarmine; on their return home they would brag about their courage, waving their certificate in front of their friends.

Bellarmine was rector for only two years. Rumors that he was to be created a cardinal led to his appointment in 1594 as Provincial of Naples. It was hoped that absent from Rome he would soon be forgotten for elevation in the curia. However, in his brief time as rector he had done much to foster learning. He built and equipped a new library, and to the delight of Clavius, issued ordinances "for the conservation and advancement of mathematical studies." He also encouraged music as a safeguard against the noonday devils of boredom and irritation. He did not have a good voice, but he played the violin, the lute and other instruments with moderate skill and was something of a composer. He also spared time to copy out motets to be sung by the students, and it was probably in his time that the college came to possess a rare book published in Venice, *Madrigals and Neapolitan Songs for Six Voices* composed by Giovanni de Macque. Even in his *Controversies,* in the third volume, he found a place under the rubric "Good works in particular," to treat of musico-liturgical questions *ex professo.*

The fame of Clavius kept pace with Bellarmine's. Through his students more than through his books his influence spread beyond Europe to India, Japan and China; many of them kept in touch with him and informed him of their discoveries, sought his criticism or submitted their doubts to him. In addition Clavius corresponded with several European princes to whom he dedicated his numerous works: Rudolph II, the Holy Roman Emperor; Frederick, Archduke of Austria; the Duke of Urbino and others. Many of his students never rose to greatness but all contributed to the promotion of scientific methods in a world in danger of uncritical adherence to *a priori* or scriptural explanations of natural phenomena.

Among Clavius's most distinguished pupils, but known only among scientists, was Fr. Gregory de St. Vincent, a native of Bruges, who later became professor of mathematics at the Jesuit colleges of Antwerp, Louvain and finally Prague, where in 1631 he lost all his papers in the sack of the city by the Swedes who burned his three large manuscript volumes on statics and geometry, which he had ready for the press. At Antwerp he founded a famous school of mathematics, and his work there on conic sections led Leibnitz to put him in the same category of pioneer philosophers as Descartes. Certainly no one disputes the claim made for him to be one of the founders of analytic geometry.

Gregory de St. Vincent belonged to a later generation of

Clavius' pupils than the more widely known Matteo Ricci, the son of an Italian pharmacist, who was born in 1552, the year after the foundation of the Roman College. Ricci started his studies there in 1575 and from a preliminary course of philosophy, mathematics, Aristotle and Euclid went on to study astronomy and advanced mathematics under Clavius, then later to the construction of sundials, clocks and astrolabes. In 1578, while still a scholastic, he set sail for India. Before leaving Rome with a draft of young Jesuits, including Rudolf Acquaviva, destined for the East, he was received in audience by Gregory XIII who, besides his zeal for clerical education, had a great vision of the Church being planted in far continents and growing up without political interference from Europeans. The pope addressed a few words, dryly but affably, to each young Jesuit, warning him of the dangers he would meet and giving him his blessing.

With the knowledge he had gathered in Clavius' lectures, the young Ricci, while at sea, began to take bearings with which he was later able to revise and complete the atlases he carried with him, the best of which drew on the imagination or on the tales of travelers for the more remote parts of Asia.

Ricci arrived in Goa at a time when the Ming Emperor had sealed off his empire from Europeans. The first Jesuit to enter the country had been politely asked to leave because he was uninvited, the second was told that he would first have to learn the language, while the third, who stole bravely ashore from a small boat, was deported without ceremony.

Ricci had not sat under Clavius for nothing. He knew that the Chinese prided themselves on their scientific knowledge. When eventually he gained entry into the country, he came, not as a Christian missionary, but as a wise man from the West, dressed not in a tattered cassock but in the silken robes of a Chinese mandarin, speaking their language with an almost perfect mastery. He regretted only that he could not alter the line of his nose or the slant of his eyes to adjust himself more perfectly to his hosts. He explained to the Chinese his horological instruments, his compasses and his glass prisms. Nothing he had learned at the Roman College came amiss. Before long he was compiling in Chinese a textbook on Euclid, a subject of which the Chinese were largely ignorant; then he demonstrated the construction of sundials and the way of making astronomical calculations. He even made use of the elementary principles of acoustics learned from Clavius. In addition to Euclid, he translated three of Clavius' books, his *Gnomoica, Astrolabe,* and *Practical Arithmetic,* and wrote several of his own, including one on hydraulics and another entitled *Western Memory Techniques.* In this last work he set out the method by which he, a Westerner, could memorize at a single reading a list of four hundred Chinese characters and then, at request, repeat them either forwards or backwards. On the walls of his house in Canton hung a great oval chart. When his Chinese guests inquired what it was, he told them it was a map of the world drawn true to scale. In this way the Chinese were made aware that other great countries existed apart from their own, and that there was an entire continent unknown to them called America. Beliefs they had nursed for three thousand years were shaken and a new area inaugurated for Chinese civilization.

A revised version of the map included much data from Chinese geographers. To meet a demand for it among the mandarins, Ricci had it printed in six strips of fine paper or on silk measuring overall six feet by twelve. It was annotated across the surface like a vast gazetteer. Copies sent to the Roman College brought knowledge of China to the West as Ricci had brought knowledge of the West to China.

Ricci died in 1610, nineteen months before Clavius. During his last years he was teaching mathematics and ethics to the favorite son of the emperor, and had won more than a foothold for Christianity in China.

When Gregory endowed the Roman College he had seen it also as a seminary for the training of enlightened missionaries for the Far East. China, India, Japan and the remoter Portuguese possessions were included in this dream of offsetting the Church's losses in the old world by conquests in the new. For him the Church was not a European institution to be planted in Asia, but a living organism able to assimilate the traditions of the East when they did not conflict directly with Christian truths. Unfortunately, he was surrounded by heads of bureaucratic departments who did not share his liberal thinking and often marred his more imaginative projects. From the very start of their work in Japan the Jesuits had quickly adapted themselves to the ways of the country, following the conduct, manners and even the pronunciation of upper-class Japanese; they familiarized themselves with all the niceties of ceremonial meals and, when one of their priests died, they gave him all the pomp and ceremony required for the obsequies of a shogun. In March 1585, a month before Gregory's death, three Japanese princes and a party of young nobles, slim and demure in their white flowing broad-sleeved coats embroidered with birds and flowers, had received a tumultuous reception as they walked with their Jesuit catechists through the streets of Rome to a papal audience. Gregory wept as they knelt to kiss his feet and said, "Now dismiss, O Lord, thy servant in peace because my eyes have seen thy salvation."

Only in India were the Portuguese slow to adapt themselves. Converts there were required to eat, dress and act like Europeans, take European names with the result that they were treated as outcasts of society by the Hindus. They were further despised for drinking wine and wearing shoes of leather, which was considered impure. The first to question these practices was an alumnus of the Roman College, Roberto de Nobili, who arrived in Goa in 1604 after being shipwrecked off Mozambique on the way.

While Ricci was winning the respect of the mandarins of Peking by his superior scientific knowledge, de Nobili was identifying himself with the Brahmins of India. Living separately from his brethren who questioned his behavior, he wore the saffron dress and wooden clogs of the Sannyasi or holy men, and followed their vegetarian diet. On his forehead he carried a rectangular shape of paste to show he was a teacher. When it was learned that he was the son of Count Pier de Nobili, a general in the papal army, he was treated like a raja. Forming a friendship with a Brahmin scholar, Sivardarna, he became thanks to him the first European to study Sanskrit, the Vedas and Vedanta. On his arrival there was not a single Christian in the hinterland of southern India. When he died at Mylapore in January 1656 they numbered four thousand one hundred and eighty three.

4

When Ignatius wrote the rules for the students of
the Roman College in the year of its foundation he was careful
to avoid detailed regulations; he preferred to set down principles of behavior which in his own community had proved helpful to the harmonious living of priests from different nations
under the same roof. Many of the customs established in his
own house were adopted by the Roman College and later by the
German, Greek and other colleges as they came under the direction of the Jesuits. An Englishman, Anthony Munday, who
got admitted under false pretenses to the English College in
1579, the year Gregory XIII placed it under a Jesuit rector, por-
trays the life there more vividly than any rule.* With few
changes the order of the day which he describes also held for
other colleges.

The students worked and slept three to six in a room, "every man with a bed proper to himself," made up of two trestles
with four or five boards laid over them and covered with a quilt-

---

*Rooms such as Munday describes can be seen today on the top floor of the Ro-
man College buildings, converted now into chapels because of their association
with Sts. Aloysius Gonzaga and John Berchmans who once occupied them.

ed mattress. On rising they prayed for half an hour in their rooms, then after Mass and before breakfast, they studied there for a period, "everyone having a desk, table and chair to himself," observing strict silence without anyone "offering molestation to another in speech."

Soon after breakfast, they made their way in pairs to the Roman College where each went to his "ordinary lecture, some to divinity, some to physic, some to logic and some to rhetoric." On their return they spent the time before dinner walking and talking up and down the garden. Two students by turns served the meal with the help of the butler, the porter and a brother, whose task it was also to look after the students' wants, such as their clean linen, and the repair of their gowns, cassocks, breeches, hose and shoes.

Munday goes on to describe a meal which is more like a festal than a daily diet. "As for their fare, trust me it is very fine and delicate," he writes. "The first messe of *antepast* (as they called it) that is brought to the table is some fine meat to urge them to have an appetite ... the second, a certain messe of potage, is made up of divers things both good and wholesome, the third boiled meat as kid, mutton, chicken and such like, the fourth roasted meat of the daintiest provision they can get, and sometimes stewed and baked meat according as it pleaseth master cook to order it ... The last is sometimes cheese, sometimes preserved conceits, sometimes figs, almonds, raisins, a lemon and sugar, a pomegranate or some such sweet geer, for they know Englishmen loveth sweetmeats."

After dinner the students recreated for an hour and then, privately in their rooms, looked over the notes they had made during the morning lecture before going out again to another lecture in the evening. When supper was over there was a second period of recreation, taken in winter sitting around a fire with the Fathers. This was followed by further study, by prayers and bed.*

---

*While Munday's account must be read in parts with reservations, one custom noted by him is observed today in larger Jesuit communities. He writes: "A table hangeth by the door, which hath a long box adjoined to it, wherein lieth a great company of wooden pegs, and against the name of every scholar written

At the table, the students took it in turn to read: a passage from the Bible, the *Martyrlogium,* or the list of martyrs venerated that day, and an edifying book. In the Roman College the custom book prescribed certain reading for the greater feasts of the year, for instance, on January 1, the feast of the Circumcision, the sermon of St. Bernard for the day, and in the evening a passage from his commentary on the Canticle of Canticles. There would also be readings from Leo, John Chrysostom, Ambrose, Cyprian, Fulgentius, Gregory, Peter Damian and John Damascene.

In all the colleges of residence the students were helped by a priest known as a *repetitore,* who was available when they came to go over the notes they had taken earlier in the day at the Roman College. The office was usually given to a young priest or a senior student. In the German College it was held for a few years from 1571 by Rudolph Acquaviva while he was doing his theology at the Roman College and by Robert Southwell at the English College when he went there as a theological student in 1581 after a brilliant public defense at the end of his course of philosophy. "He was without a rival in philosophy," wrote a contemporary, "among his fellow students at the Roman College, which is the most celebrated in the world. All can testify to that who witnessed his reputation."

Both Acquaviva and Southwell were to suffer martyrdom, Acquaviva first on the peninsula of Salsette where the Jesuits had planned to build a church. On the morning of July 15, 1583 along with four other Jesuits, he was set upon and murdered by a mob driven to frenzy by a fanatical sorcerer. Southwell, who on his return to England moved in Shakespeare's circle and had cousins at the court of the queen, was executed in London in 1595.

Ralph Sherwin had suffered there fourteen years earlier, the first of forty-one students of the English College to share the same fate.

---

in the table (which is observed by order of the alphabet) there is a hole made, wherein such as have occasion to go abroad must duly put a peg, to give knowledge who is abroad and who remaineth within."

In addition to the *repetitore* each college had its own spiritual director. Among the early directors at the Roman College was Fabio de Fabi, the last of the house of Fabius, the Roman general who by his famous delaying tactics wore down the forces of Hannibal south of Rome; also Alphonso Agazzari, the first Jesuit rector of the English College, and Girolamo Domenech, whose instructions for meditation given to the students survive. Domenech treats of the different methods of meditation used by the saints and leaves all free to choose their own, *ne si può dare un modo certo per meditare.* The spiritual notes of several students that are extant illustrate the great variety of method in prayer suggested to them.

If there was any one Jesuit who can be said to have laid down guiding principles for the spiritual life of the students it was Fr. Jerome Nadal. In the early days of the Roman College he had an important formative influence on their devotions. He was emphatic that the consolations of prayer were to be used rather than enjoyed, that they were a means not, as some Spanish Jesuits would have it, an end to be sought for itself. While he was ready to discuss degrees and kinds of ecstasy, his main insistence was on the apostolic character of prayer. He aimed to develop in his charges an apostolic dynamism on the foundation of methodical prayer, empahsizing that the students' vocation lay in the "mixed" life that combined *laudes* and *opera.*

After Nadal, Bellarmine was probably the most enduring influence on the spiritual formation of the students. His *Short Christian Doctrine* gave his weekly instructions to the Brothers, and his *Domestic Exhortations,* the regular conferences he gave to the whole community. To the same period belongs his *Explanation of the Psalms,* written explicitly to help priests recite the office with devotion. Five other treatises contain the essence of his talks to the Jesuit novices at Sant' Andrea al Quirinale. Most of these works became very popular and were translated into many languages; in fact, his *Christian Doctrine* remained in vogue until the First Vatican Council. His teaching was traditional, based on Scripture, the Fathers and medieval classics. Consequently he regarded comtemplation as the normal development of methodical meditation without giving precise meaning to the term.

Among those he guided at the Roman College was St. Aloysius Gonzaga, who was happiest when catechizing Roman urchins, doing menial tasks in hospitals or visiting prisons, exercising what today would be called a social apostolate. He contracted the plague while attending the sick and died at the age of twenty-three on June 21, 1591. Bellarmine had been his guide and was with him at his deathbed.

In Bellarmine's own student days at the college a young Jesuit priest, the master of grammar, used to gather round him in the evenings a group of devout youths who, so to speak, formed the embryo of what was to become a worldwide association. Jean Leunis was twenty-seven when he was appointed in 1560 to teach in Rome. After listening to the reading of a spiritual book, the students would join together for a period in prayer. By 1562 a small confraternity had been formed. In itself it was nothing new, for such pious associations of young men already existed in the Jesuit colleges of both Italy and Spain. The original members of Leunis' group numbered about seventy: they placed themselves under the protection of Our Blessed Lady, drew up rules for themselves and undertook to hear Mass daily, confess weekly and to receive Holy Communion at least once a month. Again, there was nothing very original in this, but Leunis went further: prayer was to go hand in hand with an outside apostolate, directed particularly to the kind of charitable works that had been undertaken by Ignatius and his first companions: the teaching of catechism, visits to the sick, to prisons, hospitals and the homes of the destitute and dying. Leunis certainly knew how to appeal to the idealism of young men and to present Nadal's principles of dynamic prayer to the junior classes of the Roman College.

Francis Coster, another Belgian, took up Leunis' ideas in the Netherlands and Germany, while Canisius propagated them in Switzerland. The Jesuits in France, Spain and Portugal did the same. By the end of 1576 over thirty-thousand students of Jesuit schools or members of their parishes throughout Europe had enrolled themselves in the Sodality of the Blessed Virgin, committed to observe the practices set down by Jean Leunis for his confraternity at the Roman College. For the sake of cohesion separate sodalities were established for groups of all kinds: for workmen, priests, ladies, nobles, civil servants. Ill-health forced Leunis' retirement just over a year after the foundation of his own society, but his work was carried on by others. In 1570 Polanco reported that in the Roman College the sodalists had their own chapel where they attended morning Mass and in the evening, after singing Vespers, listened to a half-hour conference by one of the Fathers. Before 1600 the association could claim Francis de Sales, Peter Fourier and Fidelis of Sigmaringen, later to be canonized, as members. It was said that in France the sodality of Claremont College had become a seeding bed for Carthusians, Capuchins and Minims.

While in the years between the inauguration of the new building and the end of the century many alumni of the Roman College and still more of the English College suffered violent death for their faith, there was simmering in the schools of Spain a theological controversy in which the Roman professors became deeply involved.

Between 1570 and 1576 the young Bellarmine had given a series of lectures at the University of Louvain on the relation between grace and free will, a problem tied up in turn with the burning question of predestination which the Council of Trent had left unsettled in its decree on justification. Working on the same subject another Jesuit, Luis Molina, published in Granada a voluminous tome, *Concordia liberi arbitrii cum gratiae donis* (The harmony of free will with the gifts of grace), an attempt to prove that the grace necessary for salvation, which God sees will be accepted or rejected, does not impair man's freedom of choice. In substance Molina had only expounded at extravagant length what Bellarmine had taught at Louvain and later, along with both Suarez and Vasquez, at the Roman College more than ten years earlier. On its publication Molina's *Concordia* was vigorously attacked by Domenico Bañez, a Dominican theologian, who maintained that the Jesuit had revived the ancient heresy of Pelagius, a British theologian of the early fifth century, who had made man's salvation dependent on the determination of his will without reference to grace.

Molina was denounced to the Inquisition of Spain. The Domincans demanded that he should stand trial as a heretic. The Jesuits rallied to his defense. The quarrel became one between the protagonists of the two Orders and their partisans, each side trying to demonstrate that the views of the other were heretical. The excitement spread to all the cities of Spain and infected, as the nuncio reported to Rome, both "learned and unlearned alike." Clement VIII was forced to intervene. He commanded both parties to suspend the debate reserving to himself the right of decision.

In 1597 a mass of documents—reports, opinions, judgments—originally submitted to the Spanish Inquisition was delivered to the pope who protested that it would take him a long year to read them all. In the package was a *Memoriale* from Bellarmine in which he attempted to summarize Molina's position and on certain points to elaborate, correct or give precision to it. The commission which Clement VIII appointed to examine the documents broke down. He then decided that the two sides should dispute the question before him and his advisers. The first debate was held on March 29, 1602 in the presence of the pope, fifteen cardinals, five bishops and their personal theologians. Among the three Jesuits who initiated the debate on Molina's side were two from Spain and Fr. Pietro Arrubel, a theologian from the Roman College. He was advised by another professor on the faculty, Gregory de Valencia, the prefect of studies and professor of scholastic theology. By the end of the following year, the *Congregatio de Auxiliis,* as it was called, had held sixty-eight inconclusive meetings. The strain proved too much for de Valencia who had to retire in broken health and died some twelve months later, a great loss to the college. Before coming to Rome he had revitalized theological studies at Dillingen and Ingolstadt and written the first full systematic treatment of positive theology in four volumes which were reprinted twelve times in twenty years.

During the debate Clement VIII inclined first to one side, then to the other, but the Congregation had reached no conclusion before he died on March 3, 1605. Paul V, Camillo Borghese, who succeeded after the twenty-four day pontificate of Leo IX, had himself attended the debates as a cardinal. He reopened them five months after his accession, but still two years later no decision had been reached. In August 1607 in Roman fashion Paul V, a Roman, proclaimed the eighteen-year-old controversy closed. He declared the Dominicans free of the taint of Calvinism and the Jesuits not the neo-Pelagians the Dominicans would have them to be. Each side was allowed to defend its own doctrine, but not to comdemn or censure its opponents. This was followed by a decree of the Inquisition forbidding the publication of more books on the controversy. Both sides were ordered to wait the judgment of the Holy See, which was never made.

The Jesuits celebrated Paul V's decree as a great victory for their doctrine of free will. To enable their uneducated partisans to share their rejoicing they printed and displayed large posters in the Spanish cities where they had houses and under the poster inscribed the words *Molina Victor.* At Villagarcia and other cities they arranged festive bullfights, firework displays and masked balls in order to rouse popular enthusiasm for their side. At the start of the debate Bellarmine had been the chief protagonist on the Jesuit side. But not all the staff of the Roman College were at one with him in the controversy. An old professor, Fr. Achille Gagliardi, the spiritual counselor of a large number of students, addressed to the pope a letter criticizing Molina's teaching.

Fortunately, Paul V closed down on the dispute *De Auxiliis* in time enough to allow Suarez and Bellarmine to engage in another controversy productive of an original contribution to social and political theory. In 1599, before his accession to the English throne, James I, no mean amateur theologian, wrote a treatise, *Basilikon Doron,* in defense of the claim of kings to rule directly by right bestowed on them by God. In reply, the two Jesuits developed a theory more in keeping with the new type of state that had replaced the structures of medieval Europe. Their political doctrine, taken up at the time in the Roman College and developed by professors like Juan de Lugo, was derived from the concept that the people formed the basis of political authority. "Governments derive their just power from the consent of the governed," the phrase of the American Declaration of Independence, is thought to have been taken by Thomas Jefferson from Bellarmine with whose thought he was acquainted through the writings of Sir Robert Filmer. A copy of Filmer's *Patriarcha,* or the *Natural Power of the Kings of England Asserted* was in Jefferson's library. Europe and the United States are indebted to both Bellarmine and Suarez for their triumphant vindication of conscience and law. By denying to the state the right of deciding at its own pleasure what opinions should be encouraged and what suppressed, the two former professors of the college had taken an important step toward establishing the inalienable rights of conscience.

Suarez, however, advanced further. He laid down the principles that should govern international relations and from there developed the concept of a community of nations. In an age of blind nationalism he taught that no commonwealth could be self-sufficient, but all stood in need of mutual communication and aid for their own advantage and well-being. "Although each state or kingdom," he wrote, "constitutes in itself a perfect community, nevertheless each of them is also a member in a certain fashion of this universe insofar as it concerns the human race." The law derived from natural reason was insufficient to govern such an association of nations; there was need also to introduce special laws derived from the usage of individual nations, "since just as in a city or province custom introduces law, so in the entire human race the laws of nations could be introduced by customs."

Just nine years after the closure of the *De Auxiliis* controversy a Flemish Jesuit, Cornelius van der Steen, better known as Cornelius à Lapide, was called to the Roman College from Louvain where he had been teaching Scripture for twenty years. He lectured in the tradition of Maldonato, delighting his students with topical allusions and pleasantries. Between 1614 and his death in 1637 he wrote commentaries on all the books of the Bible except Job and the Psalms. His exegesis covered not merely the literal sense of scripture but its allegorical and analogical meanings. It included also the interpretation of the Fathers of the Church and at the same time was directed to the problems of the day. He was a shy, almost timorous man. St. John Berchmans, who was a student under him, spoke of his simplicity, his

43

love of solitude and the hidden life. Prayers of his own composition occur frequently in his pages and show him as the kind of "contemplative in action" which Nadal had stressed as a characteristic of a Jesuit; they also reveal a man whose spiritual life was governed by a deep awareness of eternity, a desire for martyrdom, a devotion to the Trinity and an attachment to the saints. For more than two centuries his commentaries remained classics. They were still used as an arsenal for preachers and spiritual directors as late as the nineteenth century when an *Index Concionatorius* was compiled for their benefit.

5

In March 1611 Galileo Galilei visited the Roman College at the invitation of Clavius exactly sixty-eight years after the publication of a mathematical treatise *De Revolutionibus Orbium Coelestium,* by a Polish canon, Nicholas Copernicus, who dedicated the work to Pope Paul III. In it he had postulated a sun-centered universe in which the earth was a planet revolving both on its own axis and around the sun. The book appeared posthumously with a spurious Preface which, to avoid religious controversy, presented Copernicus' theory as a hypothesis. There was an immediate storm among Prostestants whose Christian belief was structured largely on the Bible. Luther branded Copernicus "an upstart astrologer," adding that "this fool wishes to reverse the entire science of astronomy, for Sacred Scripture tells us that Josue commanded the sun to stand still adn not the earth." Melancthon, a better theologian, was not less derisive. "The eyes," he said "are witness that the heavens revolve in the space of every twnety-four hours" and to conclude that the earth moves "is love of novelty and lack of honesty."

Copernicus had graduated at Cracow University and had taught at the University of Rome at the turn of the century

(1499-1501). Besides being a churchman and astronomer, he was also a physician, economist and soldier. His greatness consisted in challenging the scientific traditions of the centuries by formulating a new theory of the universe. He had discovered nothing new, but had devised a new system based on data already available. He had died in Polish Prussia on May 24, 1543. During his lifetime he had obstinately opposed the publication of his work and intended that, if ever it was brought out posthumously, it should be introduced by a letter written to him by Cardinal von Schönberg, who had urged him to make his views public. When the book appeared the letter was suppressed and replaced by a preface by the Lutheran Andreas Osiander.

Inspired by the *De Revolutionibus Orbium Coelestium,* the young Galileo, with the aid of a telescope he had constructed, made some startling observations of the heavens which confirmed Copernicus' theory. He recorded them excitedly in a pamphlet published in Venice in March 1610. Its full title read: *"Siderius Nuncius* (Starry Messenger), revealing great unusual and remarkable spectacles, opening these to the consideration of every man, and especially of philosophers and astronomers; as observed by Galileo Galilei, Gentleman of Florence, Professor of Mathematics in the University of Padua, with the aid of a spy glass lately invented by him, in the surface of the moon, in innumerable fixed stars, in nebulae, and above all in four planets swiftly revolving about Jupiter at differing distances and periods, and known to no one before the author perceived them and decided that they should be named the Medicean stars."

The title itself revealed a flaw in the character of one of the most brilliant scientists of the time, a tendency later to bring him into trouble—to claim more for his achievements than he was entitled to claim. The "spy glass" or telescope had been invented two years earlier by a Dutchman, Hans Lippershey, and developed by Galileo. Immediately his book was attacked by a mathematician, Francesco Sizi, but was endorsed by Clavius who wrote to Galileo on December 17 that year to say that Jesuit astronomers at the Roman College were in agreement with him.

On the strength of Clavius' letter Galileo decided to come

St. Robert Bellarmine (1542–1621)

Fr. Christopher Clavius (1537–1612)

Galileo Galilei (1564–1642)

Fr. Athanasius Kircher (1601–1690)

Fr. Kircher devised this boiler for the central heating system in the Roman College.

Fr. Kircher sketched the interior of Mount Vesuvius after being lowered into its crater.

to Rome to get the open support of the Jesuits and the unofficial backing of some cardinals. He arrived on March 29, 1611 carrying several telescopes in his baggage. The next day, Maundy Thursday, he sought out Clavius. The two had first met in 1587 when Clavius, then forty-nine, was at the height of his fame after the reform of the calendar, and Galileo a promising young astronomer of twenty-three. In a letter of April 1 Galileo described the enthusiastic reception he had received from the professors and students of the Roman College. "I had a long discussion," he wrote, "with Fr. Clavius and with two other most intelligent Fathers of the same Order. I found the pupils of these men occupied in reading, not without a great deal of laughter, the latest lucubrations which Signor Francesco Sizi had written and published against me. . . . The Fathers, being finally convinced that the Medicean planets are realities, had devoted the past two months to continuous observations of them, and these observations are still in progress. We have compared notes and have found that our experiences tally in every respect." In another letter dated April 22, he wrote: "I have been received and shown favor by many illustrious cardinals, prelates and princes of the city." Paul V granted him a long audience and before he set out for Florence Galileo returned to the Roman College which put on a public and solemn reception in his honor on May 18. Organized by the students it was attended by three cardinals, by men of science and by prelates from the papal curia and from outside Rome. Sitting on a dais Galileo was addressed as a man rightly to be numbered among the most felicitous and famous astronomers of his time. Passages from his *Siderius Nuncius* were read. And among the young students who recalled the occasion were Adam Schall, later astronomer to the imperial court of China, Paul Guldin, who as professor at Vienna stoutly defended Galileo from the attacks of his fellow Jesuit, Christopher Scheiner, and the famous Gregory de St. Vincent. In a letter to Bruges St. Vincent wrote excitedly to say that the students had elucidated Galileo's discoveries before the whole university and demonstrated with evidence, albeit to the scandal of the philosophers, that Venus revolves round the sun. Clavius died eleven months later, on February 6, 1612, having seen convincingly the need of modifying accepted scientific notions by adopting the teaching of Copernicus.

Bellarmine, now a cardinal in the Curia, was worried. The Council of Trent had prohibited any exposition of Scripture contrary to the common explanation of the Fathers of the Church, and the Fathers all agreed that the sun went round the earth. On the other hand, he was against any hasty condemnation of Galileo's opinions. He appeared to be ready to accept that Scripture was using a common mode of expression but at the same time was afraid of disturbing the faith of simple people. Moreover, he believed rightly that the Copernican system had not been fully demonstrated. The attacks of the reformers had driven the Church to defend entrenched positions and since Trent there had been no advance in the principles of scriptural inspiration. In this field Galileo was more progressive than his contemporary Catholic theologians and in many ways anticipated the teaching of Leo XIII in his encyclical, *Providentissimus Deus,* in 1893. He admitted that Scripture could not err, but pointed out that commentators stopped short at the literal signification of the words. This, he maintained, led not only to many contradictions, but could give rise to heresies and blasphemies. "For then it would be necessary," he wrote to a friend in 1613, "to give God hands and feet and ears and human and bodily emotions such as anger, repentance, hatred and sometimes forgetfulness of things past and ignorance of the future. And in Scripture there are found many propositions which, taking the bare sense of the words, appear contrary to the truth, but they are placed there in such wise in order to accommodate themselves to the capacity of the vulgar." From his discussions at the Roman College Galileo knew well that the scriptural issue was vital to the acceptance of his theories.

Galileo was again at the Roman College in December 1614. He was now claiming for his observations more than was warranted but the Inquisition dismissed the complaints lodged against him. Only after further delations to the Holy Office was he banned from propounding his theory of a sun-centered universe. In 1623 his great friend, Cardinal Maffeo Barberini, became Urban VIII. Although the new pope received Galileo in audience six times, he was reluctant to lift the ban for fear of undermining the authority of the Holy Office. However, he allowed Galileo to continue writing on the understanding that he treat his ideas as hypotheses. Between 1624 and 1630 Galileo worked on his major treatise, his *Dialogue of the Two Great World Systems.* It was obvious he had tried to prove the Copernican system. His enemies raised a storm; they convinced Urban VIII that he had been fooled. The *Dialogue* was prohibited. Galileo was made to abjure the Copernican theory and was given a sentence of imprisonment, which was never carried out. It was merely a condemnation of the Inquisition which, however it is explained, cannot be defended.

The misfortunes of Galileo did nothing to dampen the zest for scientific research at the Roman College. It was universally acknowledged before Matteo Ricci's death in 1610 that his knowledge of astronomy had made it possible for the Church to gain a foothold in China where one of the most flourishing missions in Asia was soon to develop. Many scholars of the Roman College, excited at the prospect of being sent to distant countries, took advantage of the grounding in mathematics that the college offered. On their way to different parts of the globe they made, as Ricci had done, accurate reckonings of latitude and longitude and in time sent back to Rome charts of new waters and maps of hitherto unexplored territories. Clavius and his successors in the chair of mathematics never ceased to call on their former pupils, scattered as missionaries throughout Asia and America, for observations of lunar and solar eclipses, eclipses of Jupiter's satellites and the transits of Venus, which were of great theoretical and practical value. Other Jesuits trained elsewhere also reported their discoveries to the Roman College as to a clearing house of scientific information. The Spaniard, Peter Paez, for instance, was able to write in 1615 that he had found the sources of the Blue Nile, nearly two centuries ahead of their reputed discoverer, James Bruce, in 1790.

It was, for instance, about the time of Galileo's visit to the Roman College in 1611 that Clavius received from India two letters from a former pupil, the Piedmontese Jesuit, Anthony Rubino, dated October 22 and 28, 1609. Rubino, then only thirty-three, after thanking Clavius for a complimentary copy of his *Practical Geometry,* gave his former professor information about the Brahmins who "are devoted to the study of the planets and stars, particularly of twenty-seven by which they govern and rule." He had tried to learn from them their secret of predicting the hour and minute of eclipses of the sun and moon, but had failed, because they did not reveal it to foreigners. "Two years ago," he continued, "I made in this Badaga language a *Description of the Whole World,* with explanatory notes about all the kingdoms, provinces and principal cities on earth. The Indians were astonished at it." As Ricci had done with the emperor of China, he presented a world map to a local raja.

In the Roman College itself there was no lack of brilliant successors to Clavius. Christopher Grienberger, a Tyrolese, was already teaching there at the time of Galileo's visit. After reading the *Siderius Nuncius* he had spent many nights with his students on the roof of the college, observing the four satellites of Jupiter. A convinced Copernican as early as 1615, Grienberger later defended Galileo's claim to have discerned mountains on the moon and kept his sympathy for Galileo to the end of his life. When Galileo's affairs took a turn for the worse Grienberger was unaccountably not consulted. Like Clavius he received letters from former students scattered round the world. His own contribution to astronomy was the equatorial mounting of the telescope. He was using it at the college as early as 1620 though it was not until seventy years later that the Danish astronomer, Ole Romer, introduced it into general practice.

In 1624 Christopher Scheiner, who at Vienna had been Galileo's critic, joined the staff of the college and along with Grienberger helped to enhance further its scientific renown. A most painstaking and skillful observer, he constructed several telescopes. Following the suggestion of his friend Kepler he used two convex lenses instead of the concave and convex used by Galileo. The first telescope of this kind he gave to the Archduke of Tyrol, who was less interested in focusing it on the stars than on all he could see going on from his castle at Innsbruck. When the archduke complained that everything was upside down, Scheiner inserted another lens to set the image the right way up.

While Clavius was still at work, Scheiner discovered spots on the sun. He never claimed to be the first to have seen them, as Galileo probably rightly did. In any case both were late in the field for the Chinese had discovered them as early as the year 301 A.D. without the aid of a telescope. All his time in Rome, Scheiner studied sun spots and trained his students and friends to observe them. In Rome, between the years 1626 and 1630 he produced a massive tome on the sun, *Rosa Ursina sive Sol.* He was unlike Galileo in that he never made a statement that he could not support with detailed observation, and in his classes, he always insisted on accurate data as the basis of subsequent theory. At a time when interest in the sun was restricted to a few astronomers, much of this work was neglected only to be redis-covered in modern times.

In the chair of mathematics for two periods in the first half of the seventeenth century was Fr. Athanasius Kircher, a pioneer in a number of fields of scientific research. It was with men of this kind in mind that Francis Bacon wrote of Jesuits in his *Advancement of Learning* that "partly in themselves and partly by emulation and provocation of their example they have quick-ened and strengthened the state of learning."

A German, born near Fulda in 1601, he already had a rep-utation as a scientist when in 1634 he started teaching in the Roman College. As a student in the Jesuit house at Speyer he had come across some books illustrating Egyptian hieroglyphics and from that day developed an interest in ancient history. His *Lingua Aegyptica Restituta* (1643) and *Oedipus Aegyptiacus* (1652) caused a succession of popes to use him both to restore and to decipher Egyptian obelisks. But there was hardly a scientific sub-ject that did not interest him. He made a study of magnetism, demonstrated the fascination that chalk lines exerted on hens and, in doing this, initiated an inquiry into hypnotic phenom-ena. The magic lantern, which he invented, was used with novel effect in the staging of plays at the college. His name is connect-ed also with the speaking trumpet and the invention of a common alphabet for the deaf and dumb. He also drew up the first cartographic representation of ocean currents.

In 1656 when the bubonic plague reached Rome from southern Italy, Kircher devoted all his time to searching for a remedy. With the help of doctors he examined a number of infected persons and prescribed cures or treatment; he examined blood samples and concluded that the carriers were "worms so small, fine and subtle that they could only be seen under a very good microscope." It is possible that he observed insect larvae, but not the offending bacteria. However, the book he wrote on the disease, by pointing out that it spread by contact with cats, dogs, flies and other insects, may well have helped to check its diffusion.

For more than two centuries after his death his memory was perpetuated in the Roman College by a museum which bore his name. It originated in the gift of an antiquarian, Alfonso Donnino, in 1651. Kircher expanded the original collection with curiosities of all kinds, Christian and pagan antiquities, ethnological illustrations from America and the East, amphorae, mosaics, and classical inscriptions of many periods. For a long time it was reckoned one of the most important science museums of Europe. Unlike Clavius, Kircher was a good letter writer. His correspondence fills fourteen volumes in the archives of the Gregorian University.

Apart from two years spent in Malta, Kircher was never absent from the Roman College. On his return journey from the island he witnessed violent earthquakes and volcanic activity in southern Italy: both Stromboli and Vesuvius were pouring lava into the surrounding countryside. Although during one eruption he had a narrow escape from death, he took the opportunity to make scientific observations on the cause and effects of volcanos. He waited until Vesuvius was quiet, then had himself lowered by a rope into its still smoking crater in order to see what this subterranean fire was like. His investigations appeared in his *Mundus Subterraneus* (1657) which dealt in twelve books with earthquakes, volcanos, underground animals, rivers and plants.

As a young priest Kircher had hoped to follow Ricci to China. At heart he remained a devout missionary. During his archeological fieldwork in the Sabine hills near Rome he discovered an ancient shrine to Our Lady. It was perhaps the earliest such shrine in Europe, erected in the fourth century by command of Constantine under the title of Our Lady of Mentorella. Kircher restored the shrine, often said Mass there and arranged for pilgrimages to it. He died in Rome on November 28, 1680 at the age of seventy-nine. Not only did the pope and cardinals attend his funeral, but peasants from the Sabine hills. At his wish his heart was buried at the foot of the statue of Our Lady of Mentorella.

Among Kircher's earliest pupils was Fr. Francesco Lana Terzi, who after the ordinary course at the Roman College, remained on for some postgraduate research under his direction. At Ferrara, where he taught mathematics until his death in 1687, only seven years after his master's, he invented many scientific instruments but concentrated mainly on the principles of aeronautics. His smallest publication, *Prodromo overo saggio di alcuni inventori* (1670) brought him international fame. In chapters five and six he formulated his theory of flight and described his plans for an aerial ship or flying boat that would carry men "and other required weights." The ship was to consist of a wickerwork car, shaped like a canoe and suspended from four spheres made of sheet metal. A mast in the center of the car was to serve as a rudder.

On its publication he received many objections from scientists most of which he was able to answer. In 1672 Robert Hooke in London demonstrated to the Royal Society a small model of Lana's aerial globe, but further research convinced Lana that any attempt to make a large model would be a failure because a "vessel so thin, when evacuated of air it contained" could not float owing to the necessary increase in the weight of the shell. Toward the end of his life Lana considered this difficulty unanswerable and indeed providential, because such an aerial ship would create "many disturbances in the civil and political government of mankind." He asked: "Where is the man who can fail to see that no city would be proof against surprise, as the ships could at any time be steered over its squares, and even over the courtyards of dwelling houses and brought to earth for the land-ing of its crews? And in the case of ships that sail the seas, by allowing the aerial ships to descend from the high air to the level of their sails, their cordage could be cut; and even without descending so low, iron weights could be hurled to wreck the ships and kill the crews or they could be set on fire by fireballs and bombs; not ships alone, but houses, fortresses and cities could be thus destroyed." However, some fifty years after Lana's death a Portuguese Jesuit, Laurenco Gusmão, accomplished the first balloon ascent in Lisbon: he made a paper balloon go up by means of a fire lighted in the gondola. The Inquisition saw in this the work of the devil and imprisioned Gusmão as a magician. It was only after long pleading that the Jesuits obtained his release.

6

By the middle of the seventeenth century there were some two thousand students attending the courses at the Roman College. Among the more recently established halls of residence were the Scotch and Irish Colleges, both of which had been placed under the direction of the Jesuits. Their students attended lectures in Gregory XIII's new building.

The Scotch College was founded in 1600 by Clement VIII, not so much as a seminary as a substitute for the old Scottish universities from which Catholics were now debarred. It was the pope's expectation that with a change of monarch the country might return to its former Catholic allegiance. Later, when the hope was abandoned, it became clear that if the faith were to be kept alive in Scotland, there would be needed a supply of devoted and well-trained priests. Accordingly Paul V, who as Cardinal Camillo Borghese had been the Protector of the College, converted it into a residence for clerical students. In 1616 the scholars were given three months in which to decide whether they would go on for the priesthood. All, in fact, did, influenced largely by the example of John Ogilvie, who had entered the Society of Jesus and suffered martyrdom at Glasgow Cross at the age of thirty-five on March 10, 1615 after a short missionary career in Edinburgh and Renfrewshire. The account he himself wrote of his imprisonment and examinations had been smuggled out of prison and had reached Rome the same year. The college was sited in a house opposite the Church of La Madonna di Constantinopoli in the via Tritone, and although its numbers were never great, owing to the difficulty of finding vocations, it made a striking contribution to the continuity of Catholicism in Scotland, and especially in the Western isles. Its regime was similar to that of the English College. There was daily Mass and meditation and, before bed, examination of conscience; in the morning there were two hours of lectures at the Roman College and one in the evening. At least before the end of the seventeenth century the students had their distinct dress and shoes, a purple soutane and black overcloak. By that time also the college had been put on a sound financial basis thanks to a large benefaction from Mary of Modena, the wife of the exiled James II of England.

In 1624 a small group of Irish students was housed in the English College, but disputes broke out and a home was found for the Irish by the celebrated Franciscan, Luke Waddington, near the Church of Sant' Isidore. In 1628 the Irish College was formally established thanks to the munificence of the young Cardinal Ludovico Ludovisi, the Protector of Ireland, who had also seen to the building of the Church of Sant' Ignazio. As with the English College, its students took an oath to return to their native land and work there as priests. Sometimes this proved impossible as is seen in a letter preserved in the archives of the college addressed by its most distinguished alumnus, St. Oliver Plunket, to the General of the Jesuits, dated June 1654. The cruel campaign being waged by Oliver Cromwell's army made any crossing to Ireland impossible. Protesting and promising to return as soon as ordered in accordance with his oath, Plunket sought permission to stay on in Rome in the meantime. He had entered the Irish College in 1647 and had followed the full course of philosophy, mathematics and theology at the Roman College. His rector at the Irish College, Edward Lock, testified that he was ranked among the best students and was also conspicuous for his piety, kindness and gentlemanly behavior.

Plunket would seem also to have had a remarkable gift for making friends. Among those who remained close to him all his life was Pietro Sforza Pallavicini, his professor of theology at the Roman College. At the time Pallavicini had already started on his monumental *History of the Council of Trent* which until comparatively recent times, remained the standard work on the subject. It appeared in the years 1656 and 1657, reliable throughout though polemic in parts. The volumes of documents he collected while at work, now preserved in the archives of the Gregorian University, are perhaps the most complete collection of material on the subject. When Pallavicini was made a cardinal by Alexander VII, his companion and friend of his youth, Plunket, visited him frequently and in a letter written from Ireland in 1676 recalled the "erudite conversations" he had so much enjoyed in Rome in the company of Pallavicini and other cardinals.

With the increase of students at the Roman College there was clearly need for a university church that would be sufficiently ample for ceremonial occasions. Funds were lacking until a young benefactor came forward, Cardinal Ludovico Ludovisi, the nephew of Alessandro Ludovisi, Pope Gregory XV. The cardinal, who had worked hard for the canonization of St. Ignatius, wanted to erect a fine church in his honor. His first idea was to build it at Monte Cavallo near the Jesuit novitiate of Sant' Andrea al Quirinale, but he later decided to make it the church of the Roman College.

From the many designs submitted by different architects Cardinal Ludovisi selected that of the Jesuit, Fr. Orazio Grassi, then professor of mathematics at the college. The result was one of the finest monuments to Roman baroque. The site chosen was at the rear of the college where it was necessary to demolish the small Church of the Annunziata and some offices and classrooms where the young Gregory XV, while a pupil at the German College, had studied.

The foundation stone was laid on August 4, 1626 by the cardinal. On one side was inscribed his name and the date; the other side read: *Erit lapis iste in signum meae erga S. Ignatium ejusque Ordinem pietatis.* "This stone will be a mark of my attachment to St. Ignatius and his Order." After the blessing and Mass the cardinal was entertained at dinner at the college where twenty-three short sermons were given in twenty-three languages during the course of the meal. When it was over the cardinal attended a concert in which special songs, composed in his honor, were sung. On taking his leave he expressed himself satisfied with his reception.

To complete the church it became necessary to square off the block in the way it is seen today. In 1630 the college acquired a small nearby church, San Nicolas in Forlitoribus, belonging to the Camaldolese monks and a few houses close to it. This made possible a startling transformation of the area thanks to Filippo Raguzzini, a disciple of Borromini, who designed a piazza in front of the facade in which he arranged the houses like the wings of a theater with converging streets similar to the traditional entrances on to the stage. In the course of building Grassi's plans underwent considerable modifications.

Cardinal Ludovisi never saw the church completed. He died as Archbishop of Bologna on November 18, 1632 at the age of thirty-seven. In 1640, the year of the first centenary of the foundation of the Society of Jesus, on August 7, the octave day of the feast of St. Ignatius, the church, still far from complete, was used for the first time. As it was not yet roofed, the building was covered with a large awning, tapestries adorned the nave and there was music to fit the occasion. Fr. Mutio Viteleschi, the General of the Society, sang the first Mass at which the Marchesa di Fiano, the mother of Cardinal Ludovisi, received Holy Communion.

The next day Urban VIII came to look at the church, but it was not until August 7, 1650, ten years later, that it was opened to the public at a solemn Vespers attended by Innocent X. After the service the pope sought out Fr. Orazio Grassi to congratulate him on his work.

The ornamentation of the church went on well into the next century. The ceiling and apse were the work of Andrea de Pozzo, the Jesuit architect and painter and, in his day, the unquestionable master of perspective. The altars in both transepts were designed by him for the tombs of two alumni of the college, Sts. Louis Gonzaga and John Berchmans.

Andrea de Pozzo had chosen perspective as his favorite study. In the introduction to his book on the subject he wrote: "May the reader be pleased to take up this work with joy and with the intention of drawing the lines of his subjects always to the true point of his vision, that is, to the glory of God." He laid down exact instructions for the decoration of ceiling pieces and before the end of his life, with the help of lesser architects in Europe and in China, had carried illusionism to the point of perfection which can be seen today in the ceiling of Sant' Ignazio. Goethe in his *Italian Journey* records his impression of this masterpiece of the baroque. "As decoration," he writes, "gold, silver, metal and polished stone are heaped up in such splendor and profusion that must dazzle the devout of all classes. This is indeed characteristic of the Catholic genius in the service of God. I have, however, never seen it developed with so much understanding, skill and consistency as the Jesuits have done. Everything they do is so conceived that, unlike members of other Orders, they invigorate all things with pomp and splendor in the spirit of the times."

At the time of the suppression of the Society in 1773 a large store of marble collected for the completion of the interior was carried off to enrich the churches of Sant' Antonio de Portoghesi and San Luigi dei Francesi.

Thanks mainly to the German College, the music at Sant' Ignazio on the solemn occasions matched the church's architectural splendor. In the late sixteenth and through the seventeenth century the college was not only one of the leading musical centers in Italy, but also a channel for the propagation of Italian music in northern Europe. At the end of their course students took home with them Italian musical training and techniques. From a memorandum written by Fr. González, to whom St. Ignatius dictated a portion of his life, it is clear that both the first rector and some early students were excellent singers. Ignatius himself had enjoyed music and when he felt depressed "he would call for one of the brothers or for a student from the German College, where there were many excellent musicians" to sing to him, or would summon the rector, Fr. des Freux, to "play something for him on the clavichord (while he sat in his room somewhat upset) or to sing something, since music helped him a great deal." In 1555 Ignatius had established the custom of solemn sung Vespers every Sunday and feast day at the Roman and German Colleges. He hoped in this way to make the pope content not to insist that the Society should be tied to the sung office, and he reserved to himself the right to select what music should be used in the church.

The first complete description of the musical training at the German College is given by an anonymous writer in 1611. He states that after the main meal, the most proficient singers went for tuition to the *maestro di capella*—either alone or together or in two or three choirs, sometimes learning to take a note from the organ or to project their voice. In addition it was the custom at the college to sing madrigals at recreation either in the room of the *maestro di capella* or in some other place. When Gregory XIII gave the college the Church of Sant' Apollinaire while Fr. Lauretano, an excellent musician, was rector, the Germans also had the responsibility of maintaining the church services there. Music prospered as never before, and "whatever other fame the college may have had, the Germans, because of their precise, grave and beautiful singing earned outstanding praise in the entire city." On festivals in the Roman College or on solemn receptions there or in Sant' Ignazio the Germans made the principal choral contribution to the occasion.

A great advance was made in 1564 when Gregory XIII placed the Roman seminary under the direction of the Jesuits, who took seriously the decrees of Trent concerning the instruction of young clerics in ecclesiastical music and liturgical functions. Looking round for a *maestro di capella* they engaged the composer of the "Missa Papae Marcelli," Giovanni da Palestrina, who had previously been in charge of music both in the Lateran and Santa Maria Maggiore. For a little more than a nominal salary he helped also in the Roman and German Colleges. In 1556 his future rival, Thomas de Victoria, entered the German College as a *convictor*,* a young man of nineteen who ten years

---

*A student who joined the college for the sake of its education without the intention of going on for the priesthood. He had to pay for his tuition, which helped to meet the cost of maintaining the seminarians.

later took charge of the music there. Both composers wrote for a full orchestra, with violins, lutes, oboes, cymbals and other instruments. It could well be claimed that most of the great post-Tridentine Roman musicians were not only friends of the Jesuits, but worked in their colleges and in the churches associated with them.

Sant' Ignazio had been open less than six years when the Roman College received a visit from a woman of formidable intellect, whose reception into the Church had left Catholics in Rome incredulous, even after her arrival in the city. She was none other than Queen Christina of Sweden, daughter of Gustavus Adolphus, champion of the Protestant cause in northen Europe, who had been unhorsed and slain at the moment of victory in the battle of Lutzen in 1632. She was the last of the house of Vasa. At her accession the Swedish Empire was at its greatest, encompassing all Finland and the greater part of the north Baltic littoral. In June 1654 she had abdicated in favor of her cousin, Charles Gustavus, in the great hall at Uppsala and had been received into the Church at Innsbruck on her way to Rome where she arrived two days before Christmas 1655.

Early in the new year Christina expressed a wish to visit the Roman College: she knew of the Jesuits' attempt to recover her country for the faith and she had heard of their scientific discoveries in her discussions with Hugo Grotius and René Descartes in the royal palace at Stockholm. Alexander VII made clear his desire that she should be received with all the pomp befitting her rank. For two days schools were closed while preparations were made for her visit. A baldacchino was erected above a throne set in the cortile, and between the arches were hung paintings of Christian heroines famed for different virtues, each surrounded by appropriate emblems and inscriptions. The corridors and main staircase were adorned in the same way. On the day itself, January 20, the curious crowds outside the college were kept in control by a squadron of twenty Swiss Guards. On arrival the Queen and her court were greeted by a peal of bells. Passing through the main door she was conducted to her throne where she listened to an address of welcome from the rector. Afterwards, as Gregory XIII had done at the opening of the college, she visited each classroom in turn where she was welcomed by a short poetic composition in her honor. As she passed into the church to pray before the Blessed Sacrament the choir sang motets written for the occasion. To escape being mobbed she left the college by the church door.

The Queen was there again on January 31, to look at the college library, the sacristy and paintings. She clearly appreciated her reception, for soon afterwards she gave notice that she wished to attend Mass in the church on the first Sunday of Lent. Accordingly, she took her place on a dais within the sanctuary as was the right of royal personages. Later, the Queen was to shock Rome by flouting conventions of dress, appearing often in male attire. Her authoritarian manner would frequently lead to strained relations with the popes.

A note of rejoicing enters into the college diary in 1667 when Cardinal Giulio Rospigliosi was elected pope and took the name of Clement IX. He had entered the Roman College in 1614 as a student of humanities and had gone on to study philosophy with some distinction for he made a public defense at the end of his three years. "He was a good defendant," the diarist notes, "and a good musician." Rospigliosi was the fourth of five alumni to become pope in that century, three of whom had been elected in succession; another three were elected in the eighteenth century.*

At least once a year a more solemn public defense was held at the Roman College. On August 13, 1703 the diary notes that Signor Abbate Annibale, nephew of the Rospigliosi pope, made a public defense of the whole of philosophy and theology which lasted all morning and afternoon. Twenty-one cardinals were present and one hundred and thirty prelates, as well as the ambassadors of Venice, Bologna and Ferrara and the parents of the defendant. Among the objicients were a Conventual Friar, a

---

*The others were Gregory XV, Alessandro Ludovisi (1621-23); Urban VIII, Maffeo Barberini (1623-44); Innocent X, G.B. Pamphili (1644-55); Innocent XII, Antonio Pignatelli (1691-1700); Clement XI, G. Francesco Albani (1700-21); Innocent XIII, Michelangelo dei Conti (1721-24) and Clement XII, Lorenzo Corsini (1730-40).

Consultant of the Holy Office and the Dominican Prior of Minerva.

At other times, such as prize days, the *salone* was converted into a theater. The occasion on September 18, 1721 is typical. The play was a tragedy entitled *Alteme,* written by Fr. Giuseppe Carpani, the Prefect of Studies, a theologian, humanist, Latin poet and playwright. There were eight changes of scene and below the stage an orchestra of more than thirty instruments. The play was dedicated to Cardinal D'Acugna, who had defrayed all expenses, including lavish refreshments for the guests among whom were twenty-three cardinals and seventy prelates. The play lasted three hours. In all, four performances were given and on each occasion it was necessary to call out the Swiss Guards to control the crowds that sought to get into the hall.

This was the high season of the Jesuit theater. The pageantry and equipment had become much more elaborate since the first plays were staged in Ignatius' time. Already in 1593 it had been necessary for the Jesuit General to caution rectors to see that the time given to rehearsals did not extend to weeks and months. Comedies were usually limited to a running time of four hours. At first women's roles were not permitted; if it was necessary to impersonate the female virtues, the actors were to perform in cassocks. Presumably an exemption was given for the first recorded drama put on by the Roman College in 1568, when the subject chosen was the Martyrdom of St. Catherine. In 1573 a play on the Last Judgment was such a success with its series of eerie apparitions and alarming vistas that it was repeated the following year. Only the best plays were published; for the greater number there was nothing more than a programme, which contained a general summary of the plot and shorter summaries of each act. The Old Testament stories and the lives of the saints and martyrs were the favorite themes. The German College put on its own plays at carnival time in order to keep their ebullient students in control during the festivities.

The literary compositions of Fr. Carpani won him election to the Academia degli Arcadi, an exclusive society that had its origin in the circle of poets, scientists and men of letters who used to gather round Queen Christina. Only after her death in 1669 was the Arcadia formally established. Its symbol was a flute. Only poets and scientists were admitted; the men were known as shepherds, the ladies as nymphs, each member adopting the name of a Greek in that land of dreams. Fr. Carpani attended its bimonthly sessions and there recited his Latin lyrics and thus brought the Roman College into contact with the most distinguished literary figures of Rome.

It was the tradition of the college to arrange a fitting celebration whenever a papal alumnus or distinguished personage paid a visit. Sometimes the popes would stop on their way at the Church of the Minerva to be welcomed by the Dominicans, so as not to appear partial to their rivals in the schools. It probably would be fair to trace in the interests of Clement XII, the last of the Roman College popes before the suppression of the Society, the influence of Jesuit drama and the scientific zest of Kircher which infected all his pupils. Elected at the age of seventy- nine, his eyesight was so weak that he became totally blind two years later. He was a true Corsini, with a long aquiline nose and prominent upper lip. As a youth of fifteen at the Roman College he had been no great scholar but had a reputation as a fine chess player. He was a pope in the Florentine tradition, a friend of learning and a patron of the arts. With Kircher's example before him, he created the first public museum of antiquities in Europe on the Capitol; he also enlarged the Vatican library and began the Trevi fountain, where Neptune stands on a coach formed by a shell drawn by sea horses led by tritons. It was unfinished at the time of his death in 1740.

Other popes, alumni of the Roman College, anxious to show their indebtedness to their former teachers, found occasion to create them cardinals. In the seventeenth century two professors of the college were honored in this way, Sforza Pallavicini, the historian of Trent, and a priest of very different attainments, Juan de Lugo, the last of the great names in the faculty of theology before the suppression of the Jesuits. De Lugo was a Spaniard from Madrid. Like many before him, he had been called to Rome after he had won a reputation in his own country. During his twenty years in the chair of theology before his elevation to the cardinalate, he showed himself to be both a distinguished and an independent thinker. His opinions were given out without seeking those of others in their support. He avoided polemics and pioneered the social teaching of the Church which required only small adjustments to meet the doctrines of modern popes like Leo XIII and Pius XI. In his main work, *De Justitia et Jure,* he showed himself aware of the moral problems connected with the use of judicial torture by the Inquisition. His studies ranged over a wide area. St. Alphonsus Liguori reckoned him with Aquinas as one of the great theologians of all time.

As cardinal he lost nothing of his affability. He kept for himself what he needed for a bare livelihood and gave away the rest of his modest allowance to the poor, in food, money and in medicines, especially quinine which had recently been introduced into Europe by the Jesuits of Peru and was known for a time in Rome as *poudre de Lugo.*

7

De Lugo's years in the chair of theology at the Roman College saw the beginning of a movement in France that was to divert the attention of theologians throughout Europe from positive speculation to arid controversy. As with the *De Auxiliis* dispute it started with the publication of a ponderous tome. Its author, Cornelius Jansen, a professor of Louvain who later became a devout and conscientious Bishop of Ypres, believed that he had found in the writings of St. Augustine convincing support for his contention that man was too corrupt ever by his own effort to obtain salvation and that his sinful lusts made him incapable of loving God with a pure heart. Only through the grace of total conversion could he escape from the thralldom of sin.

The book, *Augustine or the Doctrine of St. Augustine regarding Health, Sickness and the Medicine of the Soul,* which the bishop had taken twenty years to write, was published posthumously by his friend, Jean Vergier de Hauranne, later Abbot of St. Cyran, whose social connections gave wide vogue to Jansen's teaching in court and fashionable circles. From the salons of Paris it was taken up by the celebrated Abbey of Port Royal and thence spread throughout and beyond France. Wherever it reared its head, it was attacked by the Jesuits.

From the principles of *Augustinus* it followed that most men were unfit to receive Communion frequently but should rather keep their distance from the altar out of respect for the Sacrament. This teaching was formulated by a disciple of Jansen's, Antoine Arnaud, in his *De la Fréquente Communion* which was widely diffused in France. Published in 1643 it was answered by De Lugo who, unlike some of his French and Italian brethren, was against the tendency to condemn the whole Jansenist movement. He counseled moderation and wanted the Jansenists to be treated with as much sympathy as Catholic principles would permit.

Other professors at the Roman College became involved in the dispute. First Pallavicini, appointed by Innocent X one of thirteen definitors to give judgment on five propositions from *Augustinus,* found himself in controversy with Martin de Barcos, a nephew of the Abbot of St. Cyran. He was followed by Fr. Balthazar Francolini, a professor of philosophy at the college, who among other books against Jansenism published in 1705 a dialogue entitled *Clericus Romanus contra nimium rigorismum munitus* (The Roman Cleric fortified against excessive rigorism), in which he held that there was need in confession only for some act of love of God no matter how imperfect. His colleague, Fr. Giovanni Luchesini, wrote a voluminous history of the movement in which he discussed a hundred and one propositions of the Jansenists condemned by Clement XI. These two professors carried the counter-attack well into the eighteenth century when it was taken up again, besides others, by Fr. Carpani, the poet and dramatist. The list of books written on the subject by professors of the Roman College continues even beyond the suppression of the Jesuits in 1773, a sad witness to the waste of much talent that might otherwise have been employed in creative thinking.

Like the *De Auxiliis* controversy, the Jansenist movement need never have assumed the proportions it did. Voltaire had a point when he wrote: "It would certainly seem that there was no particular advantage in believing with Jansen that God makes impossible demands on humanity; this is neither a philosophic nor a comforting doctrine. But the secret satisfaction of belonging to some kind of party, the hatred of the Jesuits, the desire for notoriety and the general unrest, all these factors soon resulted in the formation of a sect."

It was only in the field of spiritual writing that the reaction to Jansenism produced some positive results. Fr. G. Battista Scaramelli, a home missionary with a theatrical style, wrote in the middle of the Jansenist trouble his *Direttorio Mistico* (1753) which treated of degrees of contemplation and of passive purification, and quickly became a classic for all spiritual directors. Later came the writings of the gentle Fr. Jean Nicolas Grou, who was born at Calais and died at Lulworth Castle, Dorset in 1803. His spiritual influence continued over many generations.

Parallel with the Jansenist movement and allied to it was a dispute that hastened the end of the great age of scholastics and brought moral theology into disrepute. A book entitled *De opinione probabili rectoque illius usu* (On probable opinion and its right use), by the humanist, Fr. Carpani, is an indication of the extent to which the staff of the Roman College became involved in a controversy that played into the hands of all parties in Europe hostile to the Jesuits.

Probabilism, a moral system which allowed a man to act in controverted issues on a solidly grounded opinion when there was a more solid opinion against his action, was a principle developed by the Dominican theologian Bartholomew de Medina, and taken over not only by Jesuits but also by a number of Lutheran theologians like George Calixtus who expressed the doctrine in much the same terms as did many Jesuit manuals. "If of two opinions," he wrote, "the one is more probable, it is not necessary to choose the more probable; the less probable may be adopted if it is supported by strong arguments or has authority."

When toward the close of the sixteenth century Vasquez added his support to de Medina's teaching, probabilism became the more general, though by no means the universal, teaching of the Society of Jesus. A correlative principle gave binding force only to laws that were unquestionably applicable to the moral case at issue. In other words, so long as two opposing views on a particular law could be sustained, no law could be said to be binding in conscience. In a century in which many Jesuits were court confessors their more lenient teaching, or rather its misrepresentation, brought them many enemies. Pascal, for instance, in his *Provincial Letters,* with his clever and wicked quotations from laxist moral theologians, fathered a powerful anti-Jesuit faction throughout France. His fictional Jesuit is made to say sarcastically of his brethren: "They disagree in many cases, but that matters nothing. Each for himself makes his opinion probable and certain. Only rarely is an issue to be found which is not answered in the affirmative by one and in the negative by another. In all these cases both opinions are probable."

Not all the Jesuits, however, were probabilists. A notable exception was Fr. Tirso Gonsalez, the Jesuit General (1687–1705), who strongly defended *probabiliorism,* as it was awkwardly called, or the necessity of acting on the *more* probable opinion. Anxious to make it the teaching of the Roman College, he brought from Spain Fr. Joseph Alfaro, who occupied the chair of theology there for many years and published several books against the more commonly held doctrine of the Jesuits. This did nothing to reverse Pascal's influence. From his deliberate distortion of Jesuit teaching in the *Provincial Letters* it followed that an opinion could be found to support any act, no matter how sordid or subversive, even regicide or a *coup d'état,* fraud, sexual license and perversion. The next step was to lay actual charges of this nature against the whole body of the Society of Jesus, which their enemies were not slow to do.

However, thanks to Clavius' insistence on the independence of science as a discipline, the teaching of mathematics in the Roman College was unaffected by the stagnation in the school of theology. Before the building of the new college by Gregory XIII, Clavius had made his observations from the roof of the old building and his successors had done the same at the new college. It was not until Benedict XIV visited the Roman College soon after his accession in 1740 that an observatory was planned on his instructions. The rector at the time, Fr. Orazio Borgondi, was a former professor of mathematics, but his early death and the troubles threatening the very existence of the Society postponed its construction until after the suppression. It was sited above the roof of Sant' Ignazio at the east end of the church on the side of the Corso. The delay in the building did not, however, interfere with the researches of Borgondi's most brilliant pupil, Roger Boscovitch, a native of Ragusa, who at the age of twenty-nine was appointed to his master's chair. "He starts where I leave off," Borgondi wrote of him. Already four years earlier Boscovitch had published a dissertation on sun spots which made his name known outside Italy. During the next twenty years as professor of mathematics and astronomy he produced some sixty books or papers on scientific subjects ranging from mathematics, optics, tides and astronomy to a technical device for strengthening the cupola of St. Peter's which was believed to be in danger of collapsing. This last work was undertaken at the order of Benedict XIV in collaboration with two French mathematicians of the Order of Minims from the Sapienza: it involved an iron brace which would contain the cupola without altering its appearance. The plan endeared Boscovitch to the people of Rome.

Boscovitch was still at the Roman College when he published the work which was his most original contribution to science, his *Theoria Philosophiae Naturalis* or, to give it its full title in translation, "The Theory of Natural Philosophy reduced to a single law of the forces existing in nature." "This treatise," writes a distinguished astronomer, "the fruit of the meditations of many years, exhibits in an eminent degree the characteristics of Boscovitch's thought. First of all, it was highly original. Boscovitch had the rare faculty of being able to free his mind from the trammels of inherited prejudices. His thinking was not hampered by current fashions or contemporary patterns of thought. Even as a young student he showed that his mind was open to receive new ideas when he welcomed with enthusiasm Newton's theories, till then very little known outside England. Boscovitch

The title page of Fr. Carpani's *Tragedies*.

This sketch illustrates Boscovitch's plan to strengthen the cupola of St. Peter's.

Brother Andrea de Pozzo designed this fake cupola for the Church of Sant' Ignazio.

Fr. Lorenzo Ricci (1703–1775)

Pius VII (1742–1823)

Clement XIV (1705–1774) from a bronze medal struck to commemorate the
suppression of the Society of Jesus. The reverse of the medal reads:
Salus Generis Humani, Jesuitarum Societ. Deleta MDCCLXXIII

in fact was one of the first to propagate Newtonianism on the continent of Europe."*

In his *Natural Philosophy* Boscovitch set out his theory of the composition of the material world which contained three principal ideas: that the ultimate elements of matter are real indivisible points or atoms; that these atoms are the centers of force; and that the force between them varies with the distance separating them. Rightly the claim is made for him that he anticipated by more than a century the birth of atomic science; in fact he has been called the discoverer of modern atomic theory, not so much because of the details of the theory as for his approach to the problem of the constitution of matter.*

Apart from its central thesis, Boscovitch's *Natural Philosophy* contained much more that was highly original on the question of space and of relative motion. He had a talent which gave him the edge over many contemporaries, for he always spoke and wrote with great clarity and precision.

There was another facet to his accomplishments. As both a scientist and poet he was elected to the Academia under the name of Numenius Anigreus, a second century Platonist and Pythagorean. The choice of the name is revealing, for Numenius, a precursor of Plotinus, had proposed the existence of three gods, the Father, the Creator and the Created World. Like Caprani before him, Boscovitch attended meetings regularly. Besides discoursing on scientific subjects, he wrote admirable Latin verse. When on one occasion the King and Queen of Sicily, dressed in pastoral costume, were acclaimed by the Academia, Boscovitch was the only Acadian to greet the royal pair in Latin elegiacs. It was also a matter of pride to Boscovitch that he was elected a member of the Royal Society and was received with honor when he visited London and Oxford.

*Daniel O'Connell, "Roger Joseph Boscovitch, Priest and Scientist" in *Studies* (Winter, 1962).

*It has been claimed that Immanuel Kant's *Monadologia Physica,* published in 1756, two years before the *Theoria* contains similar ideas to Boscovitch's but, in fact, Boscovitch had published the kernel of his theory as early as 1745 in his *De Viribus Vivis* (On Living Forces) and had returned to it again in many of his works before giving it a final and full presentation in his *Theoria.*

In the Roman College he could be testy and assertive. Although he had critics both inside and outside the Order, he also had his very staunch friends and admirers, among whom was a contemporary at the Roman College whose career as a Jesuit epitomizes the tragedy that was to overtake the entire Society.

For eighteen years Lorenzo Ricci, a Florentine, later to become the last General of the Society before its suppression, was his closest companion on the staff and his most faithful supporter. From 1736 to 1751 Ricci taught in the faculty of theology and later acted as Spiritual Director in the college until his appointment in 1755 as secretary to the General before himself becoming General in 1758. An unpublished *Vita* in the archives of the Roman Province contains an affectionate portrait of him by one of his spiritual protégés. It adds not only very human touches to a little known personality but explains how he appealed so strongly to a character like Boscovitch who at heart remained a devout priest to the end of his life. Twice a year it was Ricci's task to give a triduum to the scholastics; in addition he preached their annual retreat. The writer, without wishing to make Ricci a paragon of virtue, insists that he can think of no other priest who made such a deep impression in his spiritual conferences. In the meditations of the first week of the Spiritual Exercises "he set out the great truths with such clarity and explained them with such vibrant conviction that they made an immense impact." In the second week his reasoning was as compact and compelling "as Father Robert Persons' in his *Directory*."* When talking of the Passion it was clear "that he had experienced such tender illumination . . . that he could speak of it only with tears in his eyes."

The passage explains why a priest who had never held an administrative post in the Society was elected General in 1758 when to all the world it seemed essential to have at the helm a man capable of facing up to politicians like Pombal and Choiseul. Clearly it was the intention of the Congregation that elect-

---

The Christian Directory (1582), a very influential spiritual treatise by Robert Persons, later rector of the English College (1593–1610). An English edition, expurgated of its "Roman" doctrines by a Protestant divine, E. Buny, was reprinted over forty times before 1640.

ed him to present to Europe a Jesuit whose personal sanctity was a living refutation of the calumnies being heaped on the Order. As General, amid the incessant and mounting anxieties of his fifteen years in office, he kept in touch with his friend Boscovitch. In 1766, six years after Boscovitch had left the Roman College to build the observatory at Brera, which became one of the most advanced observatories of the time, Ricci wrote to him: "I congratulate you on the acclaim that the Brera observatory is receiving on all sides. . . . Its excellent construction is due to your direction and I offer you my warmest thanks for it."

It was the time when the long campaign of calumnies, false rumors and misrepresentations, largely inspired by the writings of Pascal, was playing into the hands of the Gallicans in the Bourbon courts bent on doing away with the Society as the first step to the establishment of an absolute monarchy. As the century had entered its second half other disparate groups were working toward the same end. The Jansenist movement along with the Probabilist controversy had partially blinded the Jesuits to the spread of rationalism which was making a devasting assault on all creeds and religious institutions. In the name of sovereign reason everything that was beyond the comprehension of man was to be eliminated, leaving no room for miracles, prayer or the divinity of Christ. An essential step to the inauguration of the new age was the abolition of the papacy which could be achieved only after the destruction of the Society, its committed protagonist. Moreover, through the extent of their educational system the Jesuits had a virtual monopoly on the education of youth: the prestige and the standard of their schools blocked the advance of the Enlightenment. In addition, their success in the mission fields from Paraguay to Peking had stirred jealousies and lost them friends when they stood in dire need of support. The campaign against them was long, diversified, disunited but nevertheless yearly more menacing as the unhappy Ricci's period of office wore on.

8

Already before Lorenzo Ricci's election as General the suppression of the Society had become a leading issue in Church and European politics. Clement XIII who succeeded to the papacy when Ricci had been in office barely two months showed the Jesuits much sympathy and understanding. Six weeks after his coronation he vigorously defended the Society in a Brief, *Apostolicum Pascendi,* and at private audiences urged Ricci to meet all assaults with prayer and patience. As Ricci's letters bear witness, he obeyed.* Furthermore, the pope warned Ricci in confidence that some of his bitterest enemies were in Rome itself. Resolutely throughout the ten and a half years of his pontificate Clement XIII rejected all attempts to suppress the Society or even to alter its constitutions. *"Aut sint ut sunt,"* he is reported to have said epigrammatically, *"aut non sint"*: "let them be as they are or not be at all." Nevertheless, the pope was powerless when stage by stage the Jesuits were expelled from one European country after another and from their overseas mis-

---

*In November 1763 Ricci addressed a letter to the whole Society *On Fervent Prayer,* in June 1769 another *On Greater Fervor in Prayer,* and in February 1773, six months before the suppression, *On a New Incentive to Prayer.*

sions: first from Portugal under Pombal in 1759, then from France by Louis XV under the influence of his Minister Choiseul, a patron of the Enlightenment, in 1764, then three years later from Spain and Naples.

Clement XIII died on February 2, 1769 as a result of the shock caused by vicious threats of his removal from the papacy, the seizure of the papal states and schism if he did not suppress the Society. It was not until May 28 that his successor, Lorenzo Ganganelli, a Conventual Friar, was elected. He was crowned on June 4 after being consecrated bishop.

Ricci was happy that a religious had been elected and particularly one whom he himself had sponsored for the cardinalate when Fr. Orazio Stefanucci, professor of Canon Law at the Roman College, had declined the honor. Moreover, he was convinced that no pope would go back on the warm approval given the Society by his predecessor, or still less burden his conscience with the destruction of a religious Order without first instituting a legal investigation of the charges made against it.

But Ricci's hopes were short-lived. When, according to the custom, the new pope received the heads of the religious Orders in private audience, he dismissed Ricci immediately after giving him his blessing. Then through a breach of secrecy on the part of the secretary of ciphers, the pope's plan for the total suppression of the Society came to the General's knowledge. Yet for more than three years the pope vacillated. As he kept himself most strictly to his own intimate entourage, Ricci was unable to make any representation of his case through well disposed cardinals: in fact, they were seldom asked their opinion on any matter, even after they had remonstrated with the pope through the Dean of the Sacred College that he ignored their existence. Even the pope's Secretary of State was kept in ignorance of secret affairs.

Timid by nature, Clement XIV wished to do everything on his own. He feared not only his cardinals, but ambassadors, the nobility, the press and, above all, the Jesuits who were rumored to be plotting his death by poison. Castelgandolfo provided him with a refuge. There he took his recreation playing billiards in the winter and bowling in the summer. He was the last pope to go riding in the Alban hills. On these occasions he wore the distinctive dress he had devised for himself consisting of a white riding coat, white boots and a round red hat. Ricci was a powerless onlooker.

Clement XIV's first blows fell on the colleges directed by the Jesuits in Rome, a useless gesture designed to placate the enemies of the Society in the hope of staving off the day of its total suppression. In February 1772 he relieved the Jesuits of the direction of the Roman seminary and closed the hostel run in connection with it. In the same year he took from the Order the administration of the Irish College; then, in a circular letter to all the bishops in the papal states he forbade the Jesuits expelled from the Spanish dominions to preach, hear confessions or to catechize. When Ricci sought an audience he was refused. He then asked for a court of inquiry and was again refused. Still Ricci would not believe that Clement would violate a fundamental principle of natural justice. The Emperor Joseph of Austria put it differently, saying that he could not see how any pope "would consent to fire on his best and most useful troops."

The date for the execution of the Brief of suppression, entitled *Dominus ac Redemptor*, was fixed for August 16, 1773. No actual charge was made against the Society. In defense of Clement XIV it could be said that he was doing little more than recognizing a *fait accompli.* "For the sake of peace in the Church" he ordered the total disbandment of the Society, asserting that in the circumstances of the day it was no longer able to serve the useful purpose for which it had been founded. The pope added that he was acting also for other reasons "suggested to us by the principles of prudence and which we retain concealed in our hearts." These secret reasons were never revealed but were thought to include a threat of schism from Spain if the Society were not suppressed. As the history of the next fifty years was to show, *Dominus ac Redemptor* did not bring that peace to the Church which the pope had made the principal ground for the suppression.

On the day appointed for the execution of the Brief a prelate, accompanied by a notary and an armed escort, knocked at the same hour on the door of the Roman College and the German, Greek, Scotch and English Colleges. The Brief was read, archives, offices, sacristies sealed and the rectors, with staff and students, forbidden to leave the buildings. When the prelate designated for the Scotch College arrived at the gate wearing no distinctive dress, the Italian rector offered him a glass of wine in accordance with the college tradition. As "honest Corsedoni," as the students called their rector, held out a glass to his visitor, the soldiers rushed in and laid hands on him. For three days the students were not permitted to leave the college; the rector was held for a longer period.* Fr. Ricci was transferred to the English College while a cell was prepared for him in Castel Sant' Angelo. The Gesù was taken over by the Capuchins, Sant' Ignazio by the Minorites and the office of the Penitentiaries by the Conventual Friars. The Roman College was entrusted to the diocesan clergy of Rome many of whom had been educated there. Above them was a commission of three cardinals, each with a defined responsibility, for science, administration and clerical education. On the whole the arrangement worked well. The cardinals appointed first-class teachers and did not exclude from the staff former Jesuit professors. Free from the anxieties afflicting the Society in the years before the suppression, the new governors made some needed improvements. The more recently established chairs of liturgy and Hebrew which had lapsed, were re-established, liturgy in 1779, Hebrew in 1781. More significant for developments in the nineteenth century the cardinals completed in 1787 Pope Benedict XIV's plan for the erection of an astronomical observatory. For some twenty years after the expulsion of the Jesuits the college continued to do well under the triumvirate of cardinals.

This might have been a crumb of comfort for Ricci had he not been cut off from all communication with the outside world. For a few days at the English College, now under the Italian clergy, he had been given the run of the building, but was soon

---

*It was a long-standing custom in the college not only to retail wine in small quantities to those who brought with them flasks in which to carry it away, but also to offer refreshment to all who wished to drink in the house "provided they were persons of decent appearance."

placed in strict custody in a room over the library: his door was almost continually locked and a guard posted at the foot of the staircase into the garden and at the main entrance to the college. On September 25 he was transferred to Castel Sant' Angelo with his secretary and five assistants, who were confined in separate cells. In October his windows were barred up. He was refused permission to say Mass or to write or take exercise or have a fire in his cell during the winter. Regularly he had to endure long examinations with the aim of discovering something chargeable against either himself or the Society. Fr. Stefanucci, the Jesuit canonist who had stepped down to make way for Ganganelli's elevation to the Sacred College, was also imprisoned, groundlessly accused of fathering a book on the simoniacal election of Clement XIV.

The pope died on September 22, 1774, a year after Ricci had entered Castel Sant' Angelo. To the end of his days he had been haunted by the fear of being poisoned by the ex-Jesuits or their sympathizers.

The new pope, Pius VI, was anxious to set Ricci free, but the Spanish Ambassador, José Moniño, who had worked tirelessly for the suppression, pointed out that the release of the General would be tantamount to a verdict nullifying *Dominus ac Redemptor.* However, the rigor of Ricci's imprisonment was relaxed. He was allowed the freedom of the fortress, while his assistants and secretary were set at liberty. He died shortly afterwards on November 24, 1775. The Spanish ambassador sought to have his body buried unceremoniously in the grounds of Castel Sant' Angelo. Pius VI, however, refused. He honored the General's request to be buried along with his predecessors in the Gesù. On November 25 his body was taken to San Giovanni dei Fiorentini (Ricci was a Florentine) across the Tiber, where it lay in state. The next day, the 26th, a Sunday, a great concourse of people, many of them on their way to St. Peter's for the beatification of Blessed Bonaventura da Potenza, paid their respects to the tragic General, who was finally laid to rest with his predecessors in the vaults of the Gesù.

It could only remain a matter of time before the forces that had brought about the destruction of the Society of Jesus were unleashed against the papacy. In the wake of the French Revolution the citizen armies of the Republic first overran the northern provinces of the papal states (Ravenna, Ferrara and Bologna, known as the Legations) in the summer of 1786, then in the following winter occupied Ancona on the Adriatic. Finally, in January 1798, the French General, Berthier, took possession of Rome. An oath of fidelity to the new civil Constitution was administered to the clergy. To the distress of the pope most of the professors of the Roman College, along with many leading canonists and prelates and the great majority of the clergy, took the oath. An exception was Fr. Francesco Testa, professor of logic and metaphysics at the college. For his refusal he suffered imprisonment in Corsica.* With his treasury depleted by the loss of the northern provinces Pius VI ordered the valuables of the college to be sold and the plate of Sant' Ignazio sent to the papal mint. The college was reduced to an even more wretched condition when the able-bodied members of the staff and the students were forced to serve in the civil guard. In the end the closure of the college was ordered. Soon afterwards, in February 1798, the pope, now eighty, paralyzed in both legs, was taken over the Alps on ice-bound roads to Briançon. Apart from his doctor his only companion on the journey was his *maestro di camera,* an ex-Jesuit, Fr. Marotti. In Valence he could go no further. He died there on July 29, 1799. Even Napoleon, passing through the town on his way back from his Egyptian campaign, exclaimed: *"C'est trop."*

On the day Lorenzo Ganganelli was crowned pope on the loggia of St. Peter's, a Benedictine monk, Barnabas Chiaramonti, Don Gregory in religion, had hurried to the piazza to watch the ceremony. He was a short man and, to get a better view over the crowd, he leapt onto the roof of an empty carriage. The coachman, turning to him goodnaturedly, asked: "My dear little monk, why are you so anxious to see a function which will one day be your lot?" The coachman's prophecy was ful-

---

*Testa communicated with his friends by means of a basket lowered from his cell. At the signal from below, *sursum corda,* he hauled up the basket with provisions and communications from his friends. Testa later became Latin secretary to Pius VII. Wiseman, p. 32.

filled. Don Gregory became Pius VII, elected and crowned in Venice in March 1800 while Rome was still occupied by French troops.* He is said to have been an irresolute man when left to his own counsels, but firm and heroically courageous when under advice he saw clearly where his duty lay.

On July 3, 1800 the pope was able to return to Rome. He did what he could to bring life back to normal. Great distress had been caused by Berthier's debasement of the coinage. The population had dwindled to some 117,000. The leading families had left the city. Money was scarce; the households of some fifty cardinals and many ambassadors and prelates had been abandoned and thousands of their dependents left without employment. However, the pope managed to re-establish the Roman College and recover some of its revenues dispersed by the French. From his own treasury he granted the college a modest subsidy. But the peace established in 1800 did not long outlast the coronation of Napoleon in Paris on December 2, 1804. In 1805 when the French occupied Ancona to the east and Civitavecchia to the west and then Naples to the south, Pius VII found himself encircled. Finally on February 2, 1808 the French forces occupied Rome for the second time. The pope barricaded himself in the Quirinal. Then on July 10 a party of French troops with scaling ladders forced their entrance. At half an hour's notice Pius VII was rushed off, without a change of clothes and without money, enclosed in a locked coach in the height of summer with his Secretary of State. He was taken first to Savona, near Genoa, then in 1812 to Fontainebleau.

At the Roman College the professors who had remained loyal to their legitimate sovereign, the pope, were insulted and attacked in the streets, harried and eventually driven out of the city. In 1811 by order of Napoleon a lycée was established in the college and another in the Gesù. The college ceased to exist as a seminary.

Without secretary or counselors, Pius VII refused to exercise his papal functions. He had to wait till the military defeat

---

*Monsignor Testa, who told the story to Wiseman, had it from the pope himself. Wiseman, pp. 21–22.

of Napoleon before he could return to Rome in May 1814. Later in the same year, on August 7 the monk who had watched the coronation of Clement XIV from the roof of a cab issued a Brief, *Sollicitudo omnium ecclesiarum,* reconstituting the Society of Jesus. When, after the Council of Vienna, the Romans lined the streets to watch wagons carrying huge cases containing, they were told, the Laocoön or Apollo, the Transfiguration by Raphael or the Communion of St. Jerome, they cheered the drivers on their way. With joy they welcomed back the manuscripts of the Vatican library, the archives of the Ministries, even the records of the Holy Office. But this manifestation of relief was hardly evidence of a return to normality.

Almost the first action of the pope on his arrival in Rome had been to repair the damage done to clerical education during the years of upheaval. The closure of the seminaries, the hostility of revolutionary governments to vocations, and most of all, the almost universal conscription of young men into the armed forces had left the Continent in dire shortage of priests.

In Rome the pope charged his vicar, Cardinal della Somaglia, with the re-establishment of the Roman College. The cardinal acted expeditiously. He recalled the evicted professors, cleared the debts of the college and reorganized its finances. At the same time, the pope restored the Gesù and Sant' Andrea to the Jesuits. It was clearly his intention to reinstate them also in the Roman College, but this was impracticable, for the Society was in no position to find a staff. For the next ten years the college was run mainly by the clergy of Rome on the lines followed in the years before the suppression. Among those who attended the courses were several young men who later attained distinction, such as Giovanni Mastai-Ferretti, later Pope Pius IX, Cardinal Wiseman, the first Archbishop of Westminster, and Blessed Gaspare del Bufalo. During the same period the colleges of residence were re-established.

Wiseman was one of the first six students to return to the English College that had been derelict for a generation. Before the Channel service had been restored, his party traveled from Liverpool to Leghorn by sea, a voyage that lasted from October 2 to December 8. After leaving Genoa their ship beat against a storm for two weeks, a man was drowned, a dog went raving mad for lack of water, and the ship caught fire. The road between Leghorn and Rome was infested with robbers. "At the wretched little hotel at Ponderd," writes Wiseman, "the coachman warned us to lock our doors and as we communicated by pantomime more than by words, he drew his hand across his thyroid gland with a most amiable expression of countenance." The party arrived in Rome on December 18, 1818.

Wiseman followed the full course at the Roman College and completed it during the last months it was still under the direction of the Roman clergy. In July 1824, in keeping with the old traditions, Wiseman, when still only twenty-one, was called upon for the "public act" or the open defense of his doctorate theses before a large audience. Four days earlier he and another student had driven around Rome in a carriage distributing his theses sheets to theologians who might be called upon to "object." There were four hundred propositions in all. The performance was in two sessions, morning and evening, and among those present were Fr. Bartolomeo Cappelleri, later Gregory XVI, then a Camaldolese monk clothed in a white habit, who glided in while the dispute was in full course, and Félicité de Lamennais, whose writings this white monk later condemned: he was a man of formidable intellect, but "in look and appearance almost contemptible, without pride of countenance or mastery of eye. He spoke with his head hung down and hands clasped in front of him."

9

In his Brief, *Sollicitudo Omnium Ecclesiarum*, restoring the Society of Jesus, Pius VII had praised the Jesuits as "experienced and sturdy oarsmen of Peter's ship which is buffeted continually by storms and high seas," and he added that he judged them "fit men to break the waves which threaten shipwreck at any moment."

The pope's forebodings were soon facts. When Napoleon escaped from Elba, Murat, the puppet king of Naples, marched against Rome and Pius VII had once more to leave the city. Then in 1821, when a Republic was declared in Naples, proclamations were posted throughout the papal states calling on the people to join four revolutionary camps established at Pesaro, Macerata, Spoleto and Frosinone. But this was only a rustle of wind before the coming storms. In the center of the storm, for the next fifty years, were the Jesuits of the Roman College.

It was not an easy task for the Jesuits to take over the Roman College in the school year following Wiseman's "grand act." Already in 1815, a year after their restoration, they had been expelled from St. Petersburg, then five years later from all the Czar's dominions. In the vast Austrian Empire they were tolerated only in the province of Poland. Both Venice and Lombardy, under Austrian rule, were closed to them. In Spain the Society, welcomed back in 1815, was expelled again five years later. In the Netherlands it was given a very limited field in which to operate. It fell therefore largely to the Jesuits of Rome and, to a lesser extent, of Italy to find a staff for the Roman College when Leo XII carried out his predecessor's intention of returning it to the Society. For the rest of the century the college reflected the misfortunes of the papacy, shared its outlook and defended its policies. During the greater part of this time the Roman Jesuits lived under recurrent threats of expulsion and even of a second suppression. Twice, in fact, during the first fifty years after taking over the college, they suffered expulsion.

Pius VII had died on August 20, 1823. As he lay on his deathbed his attendants succeeded in keeping from him news of the last sad event of his long pontificate of twenty-three years. St. Paul's outside-the-Walls, the Roman basilica to which as a Benedictine he had the closest ties, was still smouldering from a fire that had started in its cedar roof, dry and scorched through exposure under a scanty tiling.

Leo XII, Annibale della Genga, elected on September 28 after what was then considered a short conclave of twenty-five days, was a tall man with penetrating eyes, a small head and bland voice. Justly he is honored as the second founder of the Roman College or Gregorian University.* By his Brief, *Cum multa in Urbe,* dated May 17, 1824 the college was returned to the direction of the Jesuits and with the college its Church of Sant' Ignazio, its museum, library and astronomical observatory. The first academic year under the Jesuits was inaugurated on November 2. The pope was present on the occasion in company with many cardinals. It was his wish that the college should function as it had done before the suppression, with the addition of schools of eloquence and physio-chemistry. To replace the funds dispersed or misappropriated during the Republic, he assigned it an annual grant of 12,000 scudi; he also reaffirmed its privileges of granting doctorates in philosophy and theology.

---

*There is a mural painting of him, flanking that of Gregory XIII, in the aula of the new building of the Gregorian in the Piazza della Pilotta.

Now, as in the eighteenth century, there were three classes of grammar (upper, middle and lower), two of *belles lettres* (humanities and rhetoric), three of philosophy and four of theology.

But the papal states included many other universities and seminaries. By a Bull, *Quod Divina Sapientia,* dated August 28, 1824, Leo XII reorganized the entire system of higher education in the states: Rome and Bologna became universities of the first class, each with thirty-eight chairs, and another five, including Perugia and Fermo, universities of the second class, with seventeen. Moreover, he threw all the chairs open to public competition with the exception of some few that had become the perquisites of the religious Orders. To supervise his establishments he founded the Congregation of Studies. Among several halls of residence which benefited from the pope's zeal for education was the Irish College. During the French occupation it had at first been suppressed, then later incorporated into the College of Propaganda. Leo virtually refounded it. By a Brief, *Plura inter Collegia,* of February 24, 1826 he assigned to the Irish a house, formerly the Umbrian College, situated in the street Delle Botteghe Oscure, with a small church attached to it.

In pursuance of Pius VII's attempt to bring Rome back to normal the pope declared a Holy Year in 1825. For the first time since the outbreak of the French Revolution pilgrims once again flocked to Rome in great numbers. But several of them lost their lives on their way to St. Peter's in an accident on the bridge of Sant' Angelo. A mule, kicking at the crowd, caused pressure against the wooden parapets which gave way. Entire groups were tumbled into the Tiber and drowned.

During the long war years there had been no advance in theological studies in the schools of Europe. Rationalism was still rampant in the secularized universities of the fallen empire. Man, his destiny, his relations with his creator continued to be explained without reference to revelation. The old Enlightenment now manifested itself in changed forms: in secularism, naturalism and in total materialism. Even the educated were now conditioned to adopt uncritically the crude and unproven evolutionary theories of Darwin as an alternative dogma to the creation of man. Only in Oxford was there any stirring of a theological renaissance among divines of the Church of England who had been somnolent for half a century.

There had been no time in Rome for a theological recovery when the Jesuits took over the Roman College. In the seminaries and in all Catholic institutions nothing more had been achieved than their bare re-establishment. Inevitably there was a return to the old manuals, lifeless if not erroneous, reflecting a mentality long out of date. The only teachers available had been formed in the old schools. They could scarcely be expected to do more than perpetuate the dry philosophy of the late eighteenth century.

The decade following the return of the Jesuits to the Roman College was a period of expansion, re-orientation, experiment and hope. Fortunately the staff was youthful. Fr. Luigi Taparelli D'Azeglio, a son of the Piedmontese Ambassador to the Holy See, had entered the Society in the year of its restoration. Formerly a cadet of St. Cyr Military Academy he was in touch with the mood of his time. Only thirty on his appointment as rector, he was vigorous, tenacious and enterprising. He sought to bring back the teaching of the schools to the works of Aquinas, no easy task when Aristotle and the scholastics were in universal disrepute. He met with but partial success and it was only much later that the task of rehabilitating St. Thomas was completed by his brilliant pupil, Giocchino Pecci, when in 1878 he succeeded to the papacy as Leo XIII.

Beyond and outside the seminaries Taparelli's chief work, *Saggio Teoretico di diritto naturale* (Essay on the Theory of Natural Law), applied St. Thomas' teaching on the subject to the problems of his day. He can be said to have taken up the study of political philosophy where Suarez left off. For him civil government originated in an extension of paternal power invested by nature in the patriarchal head of a group of families. He outlined also a form of international organization which he called ethnarchy to which societies forming mutual relationships naturally tend. In his description of a higher and more comprehensive organization, which he regarded as the natural growth of lesser societies, he is thought to have anticipated the principles that inspired the United Nations.

In his first year as rector of the Roman College, Taparelli laid down rules for the students which became the guidelines for studies there in the next fifty years. In 1825, following the general rules, he set out interim norms for those going on for higher studies.

Four years younger than Taparelli, and appointed a year after him, was Francesco Saverio Patrizi, who first taught Hebrew and then exegesis. An early opponent of the rationalist critics he established a claim to be heard in the field of Scriptural studies after they had become the almost exclusive domain of Protestant scholars. His commentaries on the Gospels took fully into account the current German and French biblical movements. He remained a highly respected exegete during a long lifetime spent exclusively in the Roman and German Colleges. In his prudent, impartial and scientific approach to his subject he prepared the way for the liberation of Scriptural studies that was to start with the pontificate of Leo XIII.

The revival of studies was due also in considerable part to Fr. Giovanni Perrone who was given the chair of theology in the same year that the Jesuits took back the college. In his *Praelectiones Theologicae* (1835) he produced a compendium of theology for the use of both students and professors. None of his numerous published works had such a vogue. It was used in all Italian and in most foreign seminaries and by the time of his death in 1876 it had gone through thirty editions. His success was due to the way he related his teaching to modern trends in philosophical thinking. In his lectures he cited, for instance, Wiseman in the *Dublin Review,* a Boston writer, Dr. Baddeley, the young German theologian, Döllinger, Dr. Jowett of Balliol College, Oxford, the *Quarterly Review* and the *British Critic.* In the Preface to the first edition he admits he is a very young man to be teaching his elders, but excuses himself by saying that he is publishing the book at the request of his students. As Bellarmine did before him, he gave full and fair treatment to his adversaries, citing long passages from the Swede, Emanuel Swedenborg, from Rousseau, de Maistre and forgotten German theologians. Throughout the thirties he took note of the latest writings of the young Newman. When dealing with the indefectibility of the

Church, he sets out Newman's theory in a current essay that while Christ had certainly inculcated perfect unity, it was equally certain that in point of history the Church had never been one, and that after so many divisions unity could no longer be said to exist. *"Omnia permiscet et confundit,* He mixes up and confuses everything," says Perrone, as he opens his reply.

Again, as in the seventeenth century, astronomy was taught as part of the course of philosophy. The first Jesuit director of the observatory was Fr. Stephen Dumouchel, who won a modest reputation for himself in France with his scientific publications. His successor, G. Battista Piancini, once more made the Roman College one of the leading scientific schools of Europe. Besides much else, he made original studies on magnetism, on cold currents and on the torpedo, but his great merit was the training he gave in turn to his successor, Francesco De Vico, who in a short career as an astronomer won fame by tracking the celebrated comet of Halley. Many other discoveries followed concerning satellites, the atmosphere, the so-called subdivisions of Saturn, the nature of nebulae and the spots and rotation of Venus. His work stimulated other astronomers to search for new comets. From the numerous comets discovered between 1845 and 1847 eight were due to De Vico's work. In addition he undertook a description of the entire visible sky.

De Vico's clarity of exposition can be seen in the notes of the opening lecture of his course. Like Bellarmine he first defined the scope of his subject and then his method of dealing with it. "Astronomy as a science," he says, "is concerned with what can be learned about the nature and about the movement of the stars. Since hardly anything is known about their nature (that is all largely conjecture) astronomy in practice is virtually applied to the movement of the stars, with its laws and causes. And this is further divided into practice and theory. Practice concerns the knowledge of instruments, the method of using them and the manner of distinguishing one star from another." Theory, in De Vico's scheme of presentation, was likewise divided into three sections, the apparent movement of the stars, their real movement and the physical causes of their movement. He tells his class that he intends not to give overmuch time to practical observation to the neglect of theory.

With his astronomical research and his classes De Vico found time to direct the *Schola Cantorum* and was also something of a composer. Popes visiting the college never failed to admire his rendering of *Tu es Petrus.*

The restoration of the Kircher museum by Pius VII led to a new branch of study in the Roman College that was continued into modern times. Much of the original gift of Alfondo Donnino, embellished by Kircher, had been dispersed and pillaged under the French occupation. A certain amount, however, was recovered and new collections were donated by the pope and others, and the whole re-ordered and improved by Fr. Giuseppe Marchi, who was the first to make a systematic study of the catacombs. The enthusiasm he generated in Rome is reflected in the historical novels of both Wiseman and Newman.* After the first excavations of the sixteenth century, the catacombs had been largely forgotten. Marchi planned a work, which he never completed, designed to cover all Christian antiquity. Ill health made it impossible for him to do more than publish an essay on the architecture of the catacombs, but his work was carried on at the college by G. Battista De Rossi, whose *Roma Sotteranea* laid the foundation of the science of Christian archeology.

Leo XII had done much for clerical studies in a short pontificate of less than seven years. His death on February 10, 1829 was followed by the reign of Pius VIII which lasted nineteen months. While the conclave that elected Gregory XIV on February 2, 1831 was still in session, a revolution broke out in the papal states. In Rome it came to nothing, but in Ferrara, Bologna, Forlì and Modena, it revealed the strength of the anti-clerical and anti-Jesuit forces. In all these cities the Jesuit colleges were closed. The new General, John Roothaan, could only communicate with their staff through a priest disguised as a foreign-

---

*Wiseman's *Fabiola or the Church of the Catacombs* (1854) and Newman's *Callista: A Tale of the Third Century* (1856) both revealed the fascination which the Church of the first centuries exercised on their authors. Both books were frequently reprinted.

er making the grand tour. He delivered from place to place the same message of patience that Lorenzo Ricci had sent to his subjects throughout Europe on the eve of the suppression.

With the help of Austrian troops the rebellion was put down. But there was another outbreak in 1832 which was again extinguished by the Austrians. The next year the first Carlist war broke out. From 1836 until 1846 contact between Spain and Rome was severed. There could be no question of the Roman College presenting to Europe an international staff of professors as in the days before the suppression. Fortunately the men first appointed in 1824 and in the years immediately following were all young; several of them held their chairs for thirty or more years, but with continuing disturbances throughout Europe the college of necessity remained more an Italian than an international institution at least in its staffing.

But in other ways the college resumed the traditions of an earlier period. In 1837, when an epidemic of cholera spread throughout the papal states, Rome with its now growing population, suffered more than most cities. Along with the priests of other Orders, the Fathers of the Roman College offered their aid to the sick. A large number of priests fell victims. A note preserved in a journal in the archives of the Roman province of the Jesuits states that thirty-six of the staff of forty priests nursed in all 1,500 victims. The English College was converted into a hospital for convalescents. "We all lived day after day," writes the diarist of the Roman College, "in total isolation in three different lazaretti. We went from house to house, from family to family, day and night, hearing confessions, bringing viaticum, anointing the dying, reading the prayers of commendation for the soul." It was in this way that Aloysius Gonzaga had contracted his terminal sickness, but "on this occasion," the diarist continues, "not a single professor or student lost his life."

As in an earlier century Gregory the Great had ordered the litanies of the saints to be sung in the streets of Rome during a similar plague, Gregory XVI commended every religious act to bring the scourge to an end. There were special services in the churches, people were exhorted to repentance, there was a solemn procession in which the pope himself walked. As in the times of the bubonic plague certain cities were cordoned off. Rome itself became a besieged city. But the pope remained at his post, providing what aid he could from his treasury. The peak was reached on August 29 when five hundred and seventeen deaths were recorded.

The Romans were not slow to record their gratitude to the Jesuits. The Roman Senate presented the rector of the Gesù with a chalice. The people too made their gift, six large candlesticks which stand there on the altar of St. Ignatius. At the center of the relief work were the Fathers of the college.

During most of his pontificate Gregory XVI, who as a Camaldolese monk had objected on the occasion of Wiseman's "grand act," was too preoccupied with revolutionary movements to give the same attention to the Roman College that his predecessor had lavished on it. Acting on the Pauline precept that the Church should obey the "secular powers" Gregory was prepared even to counsel the Poles to submit to a schismatic ruler who denied them their basic Catholic rights. When in 1837 some four Polish ecclesiastical students came to Rome, the pope would have nothing to do with them for fear of creating tension with Russia. The Jesuit General, however, after exacting from them a promise not to involve themselves in politics, found a house for them, allowed them to use the Gesù for their devotions and arranged for them to attend lectures at the Roman College. The group soon expanded and later formed the Congregation of the Fathers of the Resurrection.

However, attendance at the Roman College greatly increased during the fifteen years of Gregory's pontificate. The Ottoman Empire was beginning to crumble. In the year after the pope's accession the Greeks won their independence. Catholics, especially the Uniates, were able to renew their contacts with Rome. Asia Minor, Syria, Palestine and Egypt were opened up to missionary activity. On the southern shore of the Mediterranean, France occupied Algeria. New missionary congregations were being founded, many of them with constitutions inspired by the rules of the Society of Jesus. Gregory XVI helped to establish them and to provide houses for them in Rome from which the students could attend the courses at the Roman College. Henceforth there was a constantly increasing enrollment from among the newly founded societies.

But the activity of Lamennais cast a shadow over the pope's reign. Following the lead given by Gregory, the Fathers of the Roman College assisted in the condemnation of his writings. In Poland, Belgium and Italy Lamennais had supported revolutionary movements. He argued that there was emerging in Europe for the first time in history a proletariat made up of the common people, peasants and artisans, with whom the political future lay. His young friends went further, maintaining that the day had come when the pope should break the traditional alliance between Church and governments and instead put his faith in the people. Gregory, who saw in every revolutionary movement a resurgence of the ferment of 1789, reacted strongly. Lamennais' entire programme in his paper *L'Avenir* was condemned in the encyclical *Mirari Vos:* state interference in matters of religion was a "perverse view"; liberty to choose between religions was "an absurd and ludicrous maxim"; freedom of the press "execrable"; separation of Church and state a "dream." Further condemnations followed. Lamennais lost his faith in Christian revelation and sought truth in the "people alone."

To have expected Gregory to have acted otherwise is perhaps unhistorical, yet it was thanks to many of the principles advocated by Lamennais that the young Church in the United States was able to make such sound progress. In Rome his condemnation, undoubtedly harsh even if its terms are restricted to their theological connotation, had repercussions that lasted beyond the long pontificate of his successor, Pius IX.

10

On June 16, 1846 the announcement that the Bishop of Imola, Giovanni Mastai-Ferretti, had been elected pope was received with rejoicing throughout the papal states. He was only fifty-four, reputed to be in sympathy with the Italian liberals and to have been looked upon with some disapproval by Gregory XVI. His early actions indicated a reversal of papal policy. He lit the streets of Rome with gas, held a garden party in the Quirinal and granted an amnesty to several thousand political prisoners throughout the states. The cry *Viva Pio Nono* could be heard everywhere. In March 1848 he went further. He gave Rome its own elected municipal government, granted a wide measure of freedom to the press and drew up a constitution for the papal states with an elected chamber capable of vetoing what the pope proposed. To many it seemed he was pursuing the very programme advocated by Lamennais. He also won great personal popularity by visiting prisoners in their cells, talking to hospital patients and including simple people in his audiences. He allowed the Jews to live outside their ghetto.

Father Roothaan, the Jesuit General, whose relations with Gregory had at times been strained, was delighted. "If we Jesuits could have elected someone ourselves, we could not have wished for a pope better disposed toward us," he wrote to a friend. The Roman College celebrated the election with an *academia* entitled "The Triumph of Clemency." On June 27 the following year, the Sunday within the octave of St. Aloysius, the new pope, an alumnus of the college and a close friend of Fr. Patrizi, visited his alma mater. The cortile was transformed into a fantastic garden with flowers and the aula decorated with paintings. In Sant' Ignazio he celebrated Mass for the students and gave them Holy Communion.

There was no doubt that the Jesuits needed a protector. In the November following the pope's visit news reached Rome that the army of the Catholic Sonderbund had been defeated by the Protestant cantons of Switzerland and that the Jesuits had been expelled from the country. An anti-Catholic mob, exulting in the victory, gathered in the Piazza del Popolo and made for Sant' Ignazio shouting "Death to the Jesuits." It was the first of the many crowds that would march against the Jesuits. Demonstrations in front of the Gesù and the college became a recurrent feature of Roman life. The professors were taunted in the streets, insulted and sometimes manhandled. However, the increased enrollment at the beginning of the next scholastic year showed that the demonstrations in no way represented public opinion in the city.

A month after the college put on "The Triumph of Clemency," the staff received its first visit from an Englishman whose reception into the Catholic Church the previous February was to have greater repercussions in the century following his death than it did in his own. John Henry Newman arrived in Rome in October 1846 and returned to England at the end of 1847 after he had been ordained priest and had entered the Congregation of the Oratory. He witnessed the popular acclaim of Pius IX and stayed to see some of the most violent demonstrations against the Society of Jesus he had considered joining.

After visiting the basilicas and the catacombs Newman took up his residence in the College of Propaganda. It was then under Jesuit direction and until the restoration of the hierarchy in England three years later was responsible for the ecclesiastical affairs of Britain. On November 7 he wrote: "Yesterday and to-

Cardinal Nicholas Wiseman
(1802–1865)

Fr. Luigi Taparelli (1793–1862)

Leo XII (1760–1829)

Pius IX was cheered in the streets of Rome after granting
amnesty to several thousand political prisoners on July 19, 1848.

This lampoon, published in Leipzig, shows Father Roothan
dressed as a fox, meeting (l. to r.) Louis Philippe of France,
Ferdinand II of Naples, and Prince William of Prussia in
London. Each of these men was expelled from his country in
the revolutions of 1848. The caption reads:
Please grant my request. May I join your company?

The storming of the Quirinal, November 16, 1849

day I made the acquaintance of the Jesuits at the Collegio Romano. There is no doubt that the Jesuits are the real men in Rome. . . . I don't mean to say how great they are, but only that they are the prominent men. The Father General is a very striking person."

Newman was hardly settled at Propaganda when he heard that "the whole American church, all the bishops, I think" were up in arms against his recently published *Essay on the Development of Doctrine.* "They say," he added, "it is half Catholicism, half infidelity." In Rome itself all he heard by way of reaction to his book was from the professors of the Roman College. "They evidently," he said, "have been influenced by the American opposition which is known in Rome—but what they say after all is not much. They admit the *principle* of development, but say I have carried it too far (judging from the bits translated for them)."

To put his mind at rest Newman made a long Latin summary of his thesis and gave it to Fr. Perrone at the Roman College. He divided it into four sections: on the left-hand side of the foolscap pages he summarized his main points, leaving the other side blank for Fr. Perrone's comments. As he stated at the head of the document, he "must not be the propounder of a new theory on so grave a subject without any encouragement to believe I am concurring in the Roman traditions." And he noted: "This is the paper put into Fr. Perrone's hands by me in 1847 when I was eager to know how far my view on doctrinal development was admissible. The criticisms are in his handwriting."

Perrone, who had often cited the *British Critic* in his classes when Newman was its editor, made some helpful observations, suggesting a distinction, giving a reference where Newman could find a fuller treatment of a certain point or expressing a reservation. In one place Newman had written that "until the Church understands this or that part of the deposit of revelation in dogmatic form, it could happen that the Church itself is not yet fully aware of its view on the matter." To this Perrone replies: "I would not myself go so far as to say this," then he adds: "New dogmas do not arise, but old truths are presented explicitly for belief in new definitions." He also queries Newman's interpretation of Suarez. "I don't think," he says, "this is what Suarez had in mind, otherwise he would be proving too much." And in another place he writes, simply, "*Optime,* excellent."

At Propaganda and on his visits to the college, Newman was appalled at the austerity practiced by the Roman Jesuits. "When I go upstairs to Father Repetti," he told an English friend, "I find the poor Jesuit in a miserable but clean room—a poor mean bed on one side, a few books on the other— and a door that lets the wind through." Repetti was the spiritual director of the college, and while he formed a close association with Newman, his austerity and that of the Jesuits of the Roman College brought Newman to the decision that their life was not for him. He made up his mind on this early in 1847. On January 26 that year he wrote: "The Jesuits, of course, are the most wonderful body among the regulars. It seems pretty clear that I shall never be a Jesuit, but I never can cease to admire them. . . . What a self-denying life is theirs, as regards the enjoyments of this world." And then later, on July 25: "I respect them exceedingly and love individuals of them so much—they are a really hard-working, self-sacrificing body of men." At the same time he believed that their very unworldiness would be their undoing. He did not deny that there were very clever men among them, "but tact, shrewdness, worldly wisdom, sagacity, all those talents for which they are celebrated in the world, they have very little of. They are continually making false moves, by not seeing whom they have to deal with."

Newman daily observed the mounting hostility to the Society. By the autumn of 1847 the Jesuits had become unpopular in the extreme, the butt of journalists and the considered enemies of the people. There was talk that the mob intended to burn down the Roman College, and there was fear that, since Propaganda was directed by the Jesuits, the mob would also turn against it. "It is most difficult to say," wrote Newman shortly before his return to England, "what will become of the Jesuits. I cannot understand a body with such vitality in them, so flourishing internally, so increasing in numbers, breaking up—yet the cry in Italy against them is great. They are identified with the anti-national party in the thoughts of the people. They are the most striking set of men—I have seen nowhere such holiness and unselfish devotion."

The clue to the conduct of the Roman Jesuits during the remainder of Pius IX's long reign is perhaps given in a phrase from a letter of Fr. Roothaan when feeling against his men rose to fever pitch early in 1848. "The Holy Father," he said, "remains firmly resolved not to issue a decree against us and we continue confident in the protection of God and the pope." Unlike Clement XIV, Pius resisted the growing clamor for the suppression of the Order, and it is understandable that in gratitude the Roman Jesuits echoed his thoughts and reactions.

The revolution of 1848 in France gave encouragement to the Italians. The mobs demonstrating in front of the Roman College and the Gesù became more violent, hurling stones through the windows. The civic guard tired of attempts to protect the Fathers. The pope advised Roothaan to send his men out of Rome for the sake of safety. On March 29 Roothaan's English friend, Lord Clifford, an alumnus of the Jesuits at Stonyhurst, called at the Gesù in his carriage at three in the afternoon to take the General to the comparative safety of the Vatican. From there Roothaan, with a Dutch passport made out in the name of Franciscus Flammand and disguised in a dark wig, traveled in the papal mail coach to Civitavecchia and there three days later embarked for Marseilles. The same day the Jesuits left the Roman College and Monsignor Canali, Vice-Regent of Rome, was made its caretaker. Some of the staff returned to their families, others went into exile, the old and sick were sent to the monastery of San Bernardo at Terme.

Several professors and scholastics left for England and after some months reorganized themselves at Newton Abbot in a house lent them by Clifford. Among them were Patrizi and Perrone. Others made their way to the United States or to Austria.

Early in March the pope had proclaimed a Constitution with a parliament of two chambers. But in the meantime the demand for popular rights was drowned in the clamor for national unity. Before the constitution could be tested a storm broke out in Rome and the pope became the virtual prisoner of the civil militia. The Swiss Guard, responsible for the pope's personal safety, had to be disbanded. On November 24 Pius fled to Gaeta in the Republic of Naples. On February 9 the Roman Republic was inaugurated.

The cardinals entrusted with the administration of the Roman College were unable to carry out their commission. The new staff appointed by them was harassed; some students came armed to schools, others were persuaded to ferment rebellion in the college, the secular professors were threatened with expulsion; one of them, Dr. Francisco Ximenes, was assassinated in the Piazza Venezia.

By a decree of March 1849 the Roman College was designated as the seat of the Ministry of Finance, but there was no time for its installation in the building. Skirmishes began between the French army and the Republican troops. The college was occupied by the military. The last days of the Republic were days of terror, sacrilege and slaughter. Priests were rounded up into monasteries. When in July 1849 the first French troops entered Rome they took possession of the college. On August 7 a fire started above the passage leading from the college to the church: incendiary material discovered in other parts of the college showed that it had been the intention of the Republican troops to burn the building to the ground. As it was, much damage was done; the great hall was destroyed and with it the frescoes of Pozzo. Only in March 1850 was the college free of soldiery. In the previous April the pope had returned to Rome no longer the liberal of his first years on the throne.

It was only after the damage done to the building under the Republic had been repaired that the rector and twenty Jesuits were able to take up their residence in the college on January 7, 1851. Fr. Perrone began his lectures on the same day, but there was one notable absence from the former staff.

Francesco De Vico had taken advantage of his enforced absence from Rome to visit Paris, London and the United States. In a long letter written from Georgetown he gave an enthusiastic account of his experiences. Approaching London up the Thames he encountered a "dense and black fog" which first appeared like a cloud on the horizon and then covered the whole sky. On his arrival he was welcomed by the President of the Royal Society, the Duke of Northumberland, "who spoke Italian like a Roman" and gave a dinner in his honor at which he was toasted "after the Queen and the men of science present." De Vico was delighted with his tour of the Royal Observatory at Greenwich, where he showed particular interest in the work done on comets. While in England he met the United States ambassador, who arranged for his crossing to New York in the most "magnificent vessel of the mercantile marine." "I had hardly stepped ashore," he continues, "when the papers everywhere began to announce my arrival." He visited Philadelphia, Baltimore and Washington. The President asked to see him and a visit was arranged for July 27. "Mr. Polk (that is the President's name),"* he writes, "is a man tall of stature, with a severe frown and completely white hair." He rose from his desk to greet De Vico and his escort and invited them to sit down around him. "Gradually he became less and less grave and more gracious. He prided himself on the fact that I had finally arrived in a country where there was true liberty. He hoped that many other scientists would become enamored of this really free American soil. They would be welcomed here with great pleasure and would find a vast field in which to sow and reap the fruit of their scientific labors. The old man discoursed on these and other subjects with warm eloquence," and indeed prophetically. Then they talked about current affairs and De Vico spoke about his travels and other matters.

The two again met on Commencement Day at Georgetown University, "the most famous university of the United States after that of Cambridge (Harvard) in the neighborhood of Boston." After his return to New York De Vico went on to see Niagara, Buffalo, Montreal and Quebec. "The new world delights and pleases me infinitely more than the old," he wrote and looked forward to describing his experiences in detail on his return to Rome. This he was never able to do. On reaching London he contracted typhoid and died in the Jesuit residence in Hill Street on November 15, 1848 at the age of only forty-three and was buried in the Catholic cemetery in Chelsea.

*James Knox Polk, President of the United States 1845–49.

De Vico, however, had seen to the continuity of his work in the Roman College. His assistant, Fr. Pietro Angelo Secchi, was back in the observatory in 1850 after having taught physics at Georgetown. One of the founders of astro-physics, he did intensive research on the stars, planets and sun and drew up the first general classification of the stars which with modifications served almost to the present day. But his fame is principally attached to his extensive investigations into meteorology based on his invention of the meteorgraph, an instrument that automatically and continuously recorded barometric pressure, wind velocity, rainfall and humidity. In his own day and afterwards he was reckoned one of the greatest astronomers of the century. His work, *Le Soleil,* published in 1870, is said to be the foundation on which all modern theories respecting the sun are constructed. His explanation of spots, faculae, prominences and the corona is substantially the same as that accepted today. He was ably seconded by Fr. Respighi, who did a lot of work on terrestrial magnetism. After the confiscation of the Roman College both Fathers were allowed to continue their work without being required to swear an oath of allegiance to the Italian state which they could not in conscience take.

After his return from Gaeta the pope gave innumerable indications of his affection for the Roman College. In 1860 he beatified G. Battista De Rossi, the "apostle of Rome," an alumnus of the college, and then five years later, John Berchmans. On this occasion the gallery was decorated with the paintings of other alumni saints, including Aloysius Gonzaga, Camillus de Lellis and Leonard of Port Maurice. Every year on the feast of St. Aloysius he sent some gift for the altar of Aloysius in Sant' Ignazio, a chalice, a chasuble or pyx. As the years passed, visits became more frequent. In 1867 he came to inspect Secchi's invention of the meteorgraph which had been constructed at his expense. His last recorded visit was on the vigil of the feast of St. Ignatius 1869.

Pius IX believed he owed his restoration to Rome to the intercession of Our Blessed Lady whose aid he had always invoked in his difficulties. Now he was more than ever prepared to give attention to the growing tide of petitions, especially from

France, for the dogmatic definition of the Immaculate Conception. This also was to become the main preoccupation of the professors of the Roman College in the years following their own return.

To Perrone fell the principal work of the preparations for the definition of the dogma, which he had already in 1847 made the subject of a long treatise, *De Immaculata B. Mariae Conceptione*. The book which was published in Rome in 1852 was singled out for praise in a Brief of Pius IX and was followed the next year by Patrizi's *De Immaculata Mariae Origine*. A third professor, Antonio Ballerini, who had been appointed to the chair of moral theology in 1844, produced between 1854 and 1856 a long historical work on the same subject. Carlo Passaglia, also a professor of dogma, took part with Perrone in the preparatory work and was largely responsible for the wording of the Bull, *Ineffabilis Deus,* of December 8, 1854. He had been a strong opponent of Newman's *Essay on Development;* in fact, his firm stand against it had convinced Newman that the life of a theologian was not for him either in England or in Rome should the chance arise. Passaglia published several works of enduring theological importance. However, soon after the reopening of the college Fr. Roothaan had to warn him against rationalistic ideas that were appearing in his lectures. "Your Reverence," he wrote to him in 1850, "has in a certain sense fallen in love with the rich erudition of the universities of Germany and Holland. But it has been remarked that after following such a method of studies your theologians came out of certain universities, Catholic ones too, full of erudition but weak in dogma and ignorant even of the catechism."

In 1859 Passaglia left the Jesuits and became involved in the movement for the unification of Italy. In 1861 he published his appeal *Pro causa italica ad episcopos italicos* (To the Italian Bishops on the cause of Italy), which was placed on the Index. He fled from the papal states and accepted the chair of moral theology in the University of Turin. In succession he edited various secular journals and for a year was a member of the Italian Parliament. Before his death in 1887 he was reconciled to the Church.

Their work on the Immaculate Conception was, so to speak,

the swan song of the old professors who as young men had taken over the Roman College from the diocesan clergy in 1824. Taparelli died in 1862, Piancini, the pioneer astronomer, the same year, Perrone in 1876. Patrizi retired to the German College and died there at the age of eighty-four in 1881.

In the space of a few years a new generation of professors replaced the old, some of them men of equal eminence, others who would carry on the tradition of the college into the twentieth century. A bridge between the young and old was J. Baptist Franzelin, a Tyrolese educated by the Franciscans of Bolzano. As a student at the Roman College he had been driven from Rome in 1848 to return in 1850 as professor of Oriental languages and dogmatic theology. In his years at the college he published an almost complete course of theology which was widely used in seminaries. He was at the height of his reputation when preparations were under way for the Vatican Council. As papal theologian he was asked to prepare a draft of the Constitution *Dei Filius* on the nature of the Church. His work was thrown out by the Council Fathers in the form in which it was first submitted. Drastically revised it was finally accepted. In the consistory of April 7, 1876 Pius IX made him a cardinal and appointed him Prefect of the Congregation of Rites.

There have been many and various estimates of Franzelin as a theologian. There can be no doubt of his high standing in his own day. Certainly he attempted to enliven the teaching of theology and give it a new orientation by applying to it the principles of other sciences. In this he parted company with his fellow professors who had treated theology as a special discipline remote from empirical knowledge. His view of Scriptural inspiration was a step in advance of that taken at Trent which had brought Galileo into conflict with the Inquisition. In his treatment of revelation he was very much attuned to the mood of the papacy. He stressed the authority of God as the heavenly source of all truths otherwise inaccessible to man, but he was far from anticipating the emphasis on the goodness and love of God found in the Constitution *Dei Verbum* of Vatican II. He cannot be blamed for being a man of his time, but on one point he touches later thought: "God revealed himself in Christ," he says, "and through Christ. And with Christ's resurrection came the climax of God's revelation."

The pietistic manifestations of religion, especially in the United States, got short shrift from Franzelin. "All those so-called Pietists," he wrote in his *De Divina Traditione,* "base their faith on some spiritual emotion or sensible interior experience which resolves itself into a blind instinct or in a fanatical manner derives its inspiration directly from the Holy Spirit." But, with all his limitations, Franzelin stood out as a great theologian among his younger contemporaries.

The definition of Papal Infallibility likewise involved in one capacity or another the greater part of the faculty of theology of the Roman College as had that of the Immaculate Conception. Although it was one of the issues dividing Catholics on the eve of the Council it was not on the register of proceedings nor was it mentioned in the Bull summoning the Fathers to the Vatican Council of 1870.

However, the year before the Council met, Monsignor Maret, titular Bishop of Jura, had caused a European sensation by the issue of his Gallican manifesto *Du Concile Générale et la Paix Religieuse,* in which he laid down that the pope is not infallible without the formal or tacit consent of the universal episcopate. His main adversary was necessarily Bellarmine. For two hundred and fifty pages he criticized Bellarmine's defense of Infallibility in his *Controversies.* The discussion was taken up everywhere, and it was only after the Council had opened that the pope yielded to the demand for a definition on the subject. As the arguments for and against the definition swung this way and that, Robert Bellarmine was invoked by both sides. Dr. Döllinger later declared that the Council "did nothing but define the views of Bellarmine."* But this was no more or less true

---

*Johann Döllinger (1799–1890), a noted Church historian and liberal Catholic, in 1861 first attacked the temporal power of the pope and later became a formidable critic of Vatican I and the infallibility of the pope. After refusing to submit to the decisions of the Council he was excommunicated by the Archbishop of Munich and later largely identified himself with the Old Catholic Churches.

than saying that Ephesus defined St. Athanasius' view of the divinity of Christ.

In these years the papal states had become the last obstacle to the complete unification of Italy. When the French troops were withdrawn from Rome on the outbreak of the Franco-Prussian war, the Italian Parliament called upon Victor Emmanuel to occupy Rome. All during the Vatican Council the pope could not bring himself to believe that he would have to surrender the city. To the last moment he counted on some divine intervention to save it.

On July 18, 1870 the dogma of Infallibility had been defined. Just over two months later, on September 20, Rome was occupied. The Vatican Council was suspended and Pius IX proclaimed himself a prisoner of the state.

The city was hardly occupied when the Roman College was taken over as a barracks for a battalion of the Bersaglieri. As the opening of schools grew near, the rector, Fr. Ragazzini, wrote on October 12 to the commandant of Rome seeking the return of the college. It was, in fact, evacuated, at the beginning of November only to be converted into a technical school and a gymnasium, which were inaugurated on December 4.

The Jesuit students left to continue their studies abroad. The lower schools were suppressed. For some three years classes in philosophy and theology were carried on precariously in a few small rooms left to the use of the Jesuits by the new administrators. Representations to the government that the college was an international institution and was founded as such by Gregory XIII were rejected. In 1873 the entire building was taken over and the college was formally suppressed. The fine library, the science laboratory and the Kircher museum were confiscated. Only Fr. Secchi was allowed to continue his work in the observatory. On November 21 that year Pius IX protested in his Bull *Etsi multa luctuosa* but he went unheeded. However, the faculties of higher studies found a new home in the German College close by in the via del Seminario. After the secularization of the papal university, the Sapienza, the Roman College took over the title of university to which it had a right and henceforth became known as the Gregorian University.

Pius IX died on February 7, 1878, the first pope since St. Peter to have reigned for more than twenty-five years. Three pontificates were to pass before the Roman Question was solved. The pope had seen clearly, to quote his own words, that "there can never be any peace, security or tranquility for the entire Catholic Church so long as the exercise of the supreme ecclesiastical ministry is at the mercy of the passions of party, the caprice of governments, the vicissitudes of political elections and of the projects and actions of designing men who will not hesitate to sacrifice justice to their own interests." His pontificate had witnessed the foundation of several national colleges in the city with the intent of forming a more "Roman" inclined clergy: the French College in 1853, the Latin American in 1858 and the North American College in 1859. These foundations and others in later pontificates added to the number of students attending the Gregorian and to the body of bishops enrolled among its alumni.

11

With the appropriation by the state of both the name and buildings of the Collegio Romano, St. Ignatius' foundation now became generally known as the Gregorian University. Its new premises in the Palazzo Borromeo were modest and confined. Once the Roman palace of the Borromeo family, the building had at different times housed an ecclesiastical seminary, the college of nobles, and more recently, the German College. It was a large somber, quadrangular structure with heavily barred windows on the ground floor used originally as protection against family feuds and later against the violence of Roman mobs. "We were hopelessly crowded," wrote one student, "and this was a special hardship for first-year men whose lectures consisted of logic and ontology by dictation."

The election of Leo XIII inaugurated a new era for the Gregorian University. Shortly after his accession on February 20, 1878 he made clear his intention of reviving Thomistic studies, at the same time expressly asking the Gregorian to give the lead in this change. In his day Taparelli had fought hard for the reintroduction of St. Thomas; it was his influence, as Leo himself admitted, that made the young Pecci a Thomist enthusiast, but Taparelli's success had been very limited. There were still professors, indeed the bulk of them, both in the Roman College and in other seminaries, who did no more than pay Thomas nominal respect.

Newman on his arrival in Rome in 1847 had expressed his surprise at this, believing that the wishes of the pope carried the force of the law. To his inquiry of a Jesuit priest at Propaganda whether the young men there learned Aristotle he got the answer: "Oh, no. Aristotle is in no favor here, no, not in Rome. Nor St. Thomas. . . . They are out of favor here and throughout Italy. St. Thomas is a great saint—people don't dare say anything against him. They profess to revere him, but put him aside."

All that Newman could find by way of philosophical teaching was "odds and ends" or "whatever seemed best." Many regretted this but no one dared go against the fashion.

On August 4, 1879 Leo XIII published his encyclical, *Aeterni Patris,* in defense of the philosophy of St. Thomas, laying down the lines that clerical training should take in Catholic seminaries. At the same time he assigned a large sum of money to the publication of a new and splendid edition of Aquinas' works. Then, in the same year, he made Newman a cardinal. However, he failed in his attempt to reconcile Döllinger to the Catholic Church. As further evidence of his wider vision he opened the Vatican archives to accredited scholars of all creeds.

The Gregorian University was the first seminary to undertake a radical reform according to the mind of the new pope. Several professors gave up their chairs to see them occupied by men brought in from abroad. Leo himself arranged that the direction of studies should be entrusted to Fr. Joseph Kleutgen, who had done much to restore Thomistic studies in Germany. However, Kleutgen soon fell sick and was succeeded by Fr. Camillo Mazzella, later to be created a cardinal. Fr. Urraburù, brought from Spain to replace the eclectic Tongiorgi as Dean of Philosophy, became a prolific writer and commentator on St. Thomas.

For the first time since the restoration of the Society the staff took on an international character.

The immediate confusion caused by the changes is humorously described by a student of the time at the Scotch College who had started his course under the old regime. "Some of the professors of our day," he wrote, "belong to the immortals—Franzelin, Ballerini and Palmieri. We older men were brought up in philosophy on Tongiorgi lines, scouting matter and form and the real distinction between essence and existence. Leo XIII changed all that. Palmieri and Carretti had to go, orthodox Thomists taking their place. It was then we had a bad time of it from the youngsters who threw the arguments of De Maria and Urraburù into our faces for our confusion."

The versatile and much loved Palmieri left for Belgium. He had held a kind of dynamism, claiming that the hylomorphism* of Aristotle and Thomas Aquinas was incompatible with the findings of modern science. His philosophy was unacceptable to the new order. At Maastricht he taught exegesis until his death in 1909; his orthodoxy was never in question. He was among the first to detect and attack the modernist views of Loisy, and while working on the commission for the new Code of Canon Law, he found relaxation in writing a commentary on the *Divina Commedia*.

By the end of Pius IX's reign the number of students had been greatly reduced. Several colleges of residence had suffered heavily owing to the punitive taxes introduced by what the rector of the English College called the "Piedmontese Government" in its effort to convert Italy into a first-class power. During an audience given to the staff and students on November 28, 1878 Leo XIII expressed his confidence that the Gregorian would soon recover thanks to its importance and prestige in the Catholic Church.

In fact, the college did prosper in the freer atmosphere. Fr. Matteo Liberatore was in the forefront of the revival as a contributor to *Civiltà Cattolica*. In his writings on epistomology he used St. Thomas to refute the theories of Locke, Kant and Spi-

---

*A term coined from the Greek words ὕλη (matter) and μορφή (form) to express the scholastic-Aristotelian teaching that all natural or physical bodies are made up of matter and form as essential substantial principles. It was used to explain transubstantiation, the relation between body and soul, and also certain points of sacramental theology.

noza and to counteract the influence of Rosmini's writings. He had an enthusiastic admirer in Fr. Andrew O'Langlin, the rector of the English College, who organized the erection of a marble bust in his honor, the work of Giulio Fasoli, which stood in the aula of philosophy in the Gregorian.*

An equally enthusiastic Thomist was the young Louis Billot, whom Leo XIII himself called from the Jesuit theologate in Jersey to promote Thomist studies in Rome. From 1885 to 1910 he taught at the Gregorian. A stimulating lecturer he had among his numerous distinguished pupils Eugenio Pacelli, later Pope Pius XII, and Emmanuel Suhard who was Cardinal Archbishop of Paris from 1940 until his death in 1949. As a writer his strength lay in theological speculation from established dogma and giving theology sound philosophical substructure. In metaphysics he followed Aquinas exactly, teaching the analogy of being, the distinction between act and potency, the real distinction between essence and existence. Only in theology did he advance curious views: for example, on the question of the salvation of infidels he maintained that from a moral point of view a very great number of them remained children and therefore on their death found a place in Limbo.

It was unfortunate that Antonio Rosmini-Serbati became at this period the target of attack by professors of the Gregorian. By any measure he was one of the most significant figures of nineteenth-century Italy. Saintly in character, an able administrator, with a genius for friendship, he began writing as early as 1826 on almost every conceivable subject: politics, ascetics, philosophy, literature and morals.* With this astonishing fertility went a great apostolic zeal that resulted in the foundation of religious congregations for both men and women. From the start his basic philosophical ideas were so vigorously opposed by the Jesuits that Roothaan, who had great personal affection for him but forbade the teaching of his doctrines, did all he could to

---

*The inscription reads: *Matteo Liberatore Sod. ed Soc. Jesu - Philosophiae Aquinatis Restitutori et Vindici - Alumni Universitatis Gregorianae - Anno Domini MDCCCXCIV aere confecto.*
*His collected works have been planned in an edition of sixty volumes and his letters in another thirteen.

cushion the attack. His philosophical system was based on the personal intuition of a universal and undetermined being which he insisted was distinct from the concept of God; in other words, he would seem to have held that man can know God intuitively and through God the reality of the world. After his death his philosophy became increasingly popular. Liberatore attacked it and, as if this were not enough, Ballerini joined in with an assault on his moral teaching which sought to apply the principles of probabalism to the precepts of the natural law. His supporters maintained that these two Jesuits misrepresented his doctrines. Whether this was the case or not, forty propositions taken from his prolific writings were condemned by Leo XIII in 1887, thirty-two years after his death. Understandably the action caused harsh feelings toward the Jesuits in the congregations he had founded.

In different forms Rosmini's ideas had always appealed to more mystically inclined philosophers and in his own day had the additional attraction of providing an ordered system in place of the "bits and pieces" then taught in the schools. Newman had appreciated this when he stopped at Milan on his way to Rome in 1846: "We heard," he said, "that Rosmini's one idea was to make a positive substantive philosophy instead of answering objections in a petty way and being no more than negative. He seemed to think that the age required a philosophy, for at present there was none."

Leo's hopes for an increased enrollment were soon realized: from four hundred and fifteen in 1880, the second year of his pontificate, it grew to over a thousand before the end of the century. Some twenty different nationalities were represented among the students and also almost all the religious congregations and seminaries in Rome. After the upheavals earlier in the century the Gregorian had become once again an international university in the heart of Catholic Christendom.

Although Leo XIII avoided confrontation with the state, it is said, perhaps with insufficient authority, that he left the Vatican only once during his pontificate, and that on the day after his election when he went *incognito* to his former residence, the Falconieri Palace, to collect his papers and to return the same day. But the attitude of the city and country remained violently anti-clerical. Tablets, busts and statues were erected everywhere to men who had written or fought for the unification of Italy; streets and piazzas were renamed after them. In 1893 some anti-clerical Roman official came across Taparelli's popular treatise on human rights. "The title was enough to guarantee the anti-clericalism of the author," wrote a student of the English College at the time. "It was therefore decreed that a marble statue should be raised to his memory. The site was to be the Piazzetta of Sant' Andrea della Valle and we watched the erection day by day as we passed it on our way to the Greg." Only when the statue was ready for unveiling was it discovered that Taparelli, far from being an anti-clerical, was in fact a priest and a former professor of the Roman College.*

Two years before his death by a decree of the Congregation of Studies, dated August 16, 1876, Pius IX had formally founded a faculty of Canon Law in the Gregorian University. At the start the subject had been taught as part of the general theological course and had received notable contributions mainly from Suarez and De Lugo. Later, in 1695, it had been established as a discipline in its own right but the chair survived less than nine years for Leo XII had suppressed it at the insistence of the Sapienza which feared its rivalry. It had been set up again successfully in 1838. With the secularization of the Sapienza in 1870 Pius IX was able to found a faculty with four chairs. To direct its work the pope summoned from the English theologate Fr. Francis Xavier Wernz and it was thanks largely to him that the Gregorian was to play such an important part in the development of the subject during the next forty years.

Wernz held the chair himself for twenty-four years, lecturing daily to the students specializing in canonical studies. He was appointed rector in 1904 but still continued his lectures. Only when he was elected General of the Society in 1906 did he leave the Gregorian, but by then he had transformed the teach-

---

Venerabile, May 1945. The mistake is understandable for a relative of Fr. Taparelli D'Azeglio, Massimo D'Azeglio, was a well-known politician at the time of the unification of Italy.

ing of the subject in all the seminaries of Europe and America. On his first taking the chair, the groundwork of canon law was much the same as it had been in the Middle Ages—decretals, cases, replies of the Holy See. Into this amorphous mass of jurisprudence Wernz brought some order in his great work, the *Ius Decretalium,* which he divided into four sections: source of law, the relation between Church and state, the constitutional law of the Church, and its administrative law. The treatment ran into six volumes and prepared the way for the promulgation of the Code of Canon Law brought out by Benedict XV in 1917. Unlike many of his successors Wernz was careful always to keep clear the distinction between canon law and moral theology.

For his work on canon law Wernz received the warm congratulations of Leo XIII and Giuseppe Sarto, who had succeeded Leo as Pius X on August 4, 1903. But in the other matters Wernz and the new pope frequently found themselves at odds.

The modernist movement reared its head at the time Leo XIII's liberating policy was giving new inspiration to ecclesiastical studies. Like Jansenism it was both a movement and a doctrine or, more accurately, an approach to doctrine. Its leaders were two men of contrasting character and complementary interests, Alfred Loisy and George Tyrrell. They sought to rejuvenate the Church from within. Consequently, the extent and strength of the movement were always difficult to determine and depended on the yardstick used to measure orthodoxy or divergence from it.

Loisy, a teacher at the Institut Catholique in Paris until 1893, did not hold with the unchangeable truth of revelation in the New Testament. His most important book, *L'Evangile et l'Église,* set out a theory of development which virtually undermined the entire dogmatic foundation of the faith: all teaching, he maintained, was conditioned and limited by the times, including the message of Christ; in other words, there was no distinction between development and change. That would seem to have been at the heart of the heresy which was rendered more dangerous because it was Loisy's technique, as well as Tyrrell's, to appear loyal members of the Church and remain within its visible unity.

Tyrrell was a man of different talents. A convert Irishman he came into the Catholic Church and the Society of Jesus via High Anglicanism to find himself teaching at the seminary of the English province at Stonyhurst. As a writer of English prose he was comparable to Newman at his best. Moody, mercurial and wayward, he manifested in his last years as a Jesuit the first symptoms of Bright's disease which in part might explain his conduct. With greater subtlety than Loisy he also held that dogma was relative to the age and had to be reshaped by each generation in terms of its own.*

At the Gregorian, Billot was the leading opponent of modernism. When Pius X made his denunciation of the movement in his encyclical *Pascendi Gregis* in 1907 not only were Billot's ideas incorporated, but many excerpts from his works could be recognized in its phrasing.

The encyclical was undoubtedly necessary. Pius X was right in admitting that it had never been more urgent to take drastic measures to safeguard orthodoxy. At the same time the pope laid down certain principles which for two generations put the shackles on theological development in Rome, France and elsewhere: scholastic philosophy was to be the basis of all sacerdotal studies; there was to be strict censorship of the opinions of all professors; bishops were to appoint censors to examine all books and periodicals; vigilance committees were to be set up in every diocese to collect evidence of modernistic writing or teaching; every three years bishops were to report to Rome under oath on doctrines current among their clergy.

It can be questioned whether *Pascendi Gregis* effectively put an end to modernism. Inevitably there followed groundless delations, false accusations and untold suffering. Many Jesuits of a younger generation who might have made their mark as writ-

---

*Reckoned the ugliest man in the English Province, Tyrrell won many friends through his undoubted charm. After he was dismissed from the Society he retained the affection of his former pupils, who regretted only his duplicity toward his superiors who had done their utmost to protect and help him. While writing seemingly orthodox articles in one journal under his own name, he published surreptitiously his modernistic views in other places under a pseudonym.

ers or theologians found safer outlets for their talents. Only recent research has shown that, more than the pope, his advisers and the lesser men in his curia were responsible for a widespread heresy hunt that on occasion caught up with men totally innocent and even ignorant of the meaning of modernism.

12

The encyclical *Pascendi Gregis,* while causing wide distress, might be said to have occasioned the foundation of an institute which, at least in its original staffing, could be considered an offshoot of the Gregorian University. Although from the start it existed in its own right, it later came to be associated with its parent body in a consortium of academic institutions under the direction of the Jesuit General in Rome. To trace its origins it is necessary to go back to the last decade of Leo XIII's pontificate.

On November 18, 1893 Leo XIII, disturbed by the widespread movement in Germany to study the Bible without reference to revelation or divine inspiration, published his encyclical *Providentissimus Deus,* in which he laid down the principles to be followed by Catholic scholars in the interpretation of Scripture. It was an enlightened document designed to meet the challenge of emerging sciences to the truth of the Bible. It took account of advances in archeological and topographical research and of philological discoveries, all of which had given rise to new biblical problems. Leo pointed out the need for specialized biblical studies distinct from the ordinary courses given in the seminaries. He had in mind, in particular, the contribution that could be made in this field by the Gregorian University.

Nothing further was done for another nine years. By an apostolic letter, *Vigilantiae,* of October 30, 1902, Leo once again expressing his fear that certain trends in biblical interpretation would destroy the supernatural character of the Scriptures, set up in Rome the Pontifical Biblical Commission, consisting of a number of cardinals assisted by a body of expert consultants. At the same time, the pope expressed a wish to found in Rome a Biblical Athenaeum and, in fact, drew up and had printed for it a full constitution. But he died on July 20, 1903 before a start on the project could be made.

Leo XIII's appointment of the Franciscan, Fr. David Fleming, as secretary to the commission, his choice of forty-one consultors from more progressive scholars, and his initial intention of making the *Revue Biblique* of the Jerusalem Dominicans its official organ, all combined to show beyond doubt that his intention was constructive and not restrictive, in spite of the fact that he meant the commission to exercise also a measure of censorship on biblical publications.

Pius X, taking up Leo's plans immediately after his accession, gave the commission the right to confer doctorate degrees in Scripture. By doing this he prepared the way for the foundation of the Biblical Institute conceived by his predecessor. It can be said to have started in October 1908 when Fr. Wernz, with the help of the Holy See, instituted at the Gregorian University advanced courses in Scripture under Fr. Luciano Mechineau and Leopold Fonck. Fr. Mechineau had soon to retire in bad health. Nevertheless Pius X went ahead. On May 7, 1909, by his letter *Vinea Electa,* he formally established the Pontifical Biblical Institute, with a charter to promote sound biblical teaching to combat "false, erroneous and heretical views, especially those recently current." The means outlined for this end were, first, lectures and research into special areas of study—archeology, history and philology, second, the establishment of a biblical library, and third, publications under the direct supervision of the Holy See. All questions of grave importance were to be referred to the Biblical Commission to which an annual report was also to be rendered.

Overall the foundation of the Biblical Institute represented a positive reaction on the part of Rome to the modernism of Loisy. To some extent also it was considered by some a safeguard against what then seemed the potentially dangerous but brilliant work undertaken by the most eminent Scripture scholar of his day, the Dominican Fr. Marie Joseph Lagrange. At the end of the nineteenth century he and his brethren had founded in Jerusalem the École Biblique with its accompanying journal, the *Revue Biblique,* which for a long time was the only Catholic periodical which in point of scholarship could stand comparison with the English, German and Scandinavian scriptural journals.

However, no money could be advanced by the pope to assist the institute. The earthquake at Messina on December 28 of the previous year had exhausted the papal treasury. It had occurred at 5:20 in the morning when most of the population was shut in their homes. Besides destroying ninety percent of the buildings, it had killed more than thirty thousand people.

Three weeks after founding the institute, Pius X formally entrusted its direction to the Society of Jesus; then on June 11 following he nominated Fr. Leopold Fonck of the Gregorian University its first president. Fonck was both pious and conservative, two qualities that appealed to Pius X, whose close friend he was known to be. He believed, for instance, in the authenticity of the house of Loretto and regarded Lagrange as a dangerous innovator, if not a suspect modernist. As a scholar he was "safe," but not of the same caliber as Lagrange whose principles of scriptural exegesis were later to be universally accepted. Understandably the Dominicans feared that the influence of Fonck in Rome would restrict the legitimate progress they were making in the field of Scripture studies. Nor was Fonck the man to allay misconceptions. However, without his enthusiasm and tireless efforts on its behalf, the Biblical Institute would never have prospered.

It was the business of Fonck to find the staff, the finance and a suitable building, not to mention a library for the institute.

With the help of Wernz he enlisted a dozen experts in various fields of scriptural study, most of whom had received their training in the Oriental faculty of the Jesuit University at Beirut: Joseph Neyrand, who taught Hebrew for many years; Albert Vaccari, who was to remain on the staff for half a century and in his time produce a distinguished translation of the Bible into Italian; Anthony Deïmel, the assyriologist; Ladislaus Szcepanski, the Pole, who taught biblical geography and archeology, a prolific writer on the subjects in four different languages; and Francis Ehrle, a German, who took classes in Latin and Greek paleography and continued his work at the institute after he had been created cardinal and placed in charge of the Vatican archives in 1922. Altogether in the first year of its existence there were eleven professors drawn from nine provinces of the Society whose lectures were attended by one hundred and seventeen students.

If any of these pioneers deserves special notice it is perhaps Fr. Anton Deimel from Olpe in Westphalia, who joined the staff of the institute on its foundation and remained there until his death in 1954 in his eighty-ninth year. An alumnus of the German College, he had taught Scripture at St. Bueno's, the theologate of the English Jesuits, from 1901 to 1903 and also from 1907 to 1909 in the papal seminary of Anagni. Between these appointments he had begun at the British museum what was to prove a lifelong study of cuneiform literature.

Among his first published works were several manuals on the Mesopotamian cultures, a complete edition of the Babylonian epic of creation and his *Pantheon Babylonicum,* a classic which traced from cuneiform texts the names of the Babylonian gods. As a leading Sumerian specialist he was called to the museum of Berlin to interpret and edit ancient texts found at Fara, the city of the Flood. His pupils included Fr. Eric Burrows, who published the ancient texts found at Ur by Sir Charles Leonard Woolley, and Nikolaus Schneider, rightly recognized as the pioneer scholar of the economic and administrative history of the late Sumerian period.

Deimel's monumental work was his *Sumerian Lexicon*, published in nine large volumes between 1925 and 1950. It made it possible for the learned world to translate texts which extended back to 3000 B.C. the horizon of world literature. His achievement was astonishing for a man who never enjoyed good health and it did much to make known the work of the institute among students of the Bible in all countries. In his own community he was greatly loved as a man and was much sought after in Rome as a spiritual director.

At the start the institute had no power to confer degrees. By its charter it was to prepare postgraduate students for examination by the Biblical Commission which would award diplomas. The course of studies was planned on a three-year basis.

In its first year the institute had no house of its own. Some lectures were held in the Gregorian, others in two other large rooms put at its disposal by the Leonine College, which also gave Fonck a third room for a library and yet another for the staff. The professors found lodgings wherever they could. Fonck sent out letters of appeal for money. One such letter came into the hands of a Jesuit missionary in Madagascar, Fr. du Coëtlosquet. He put Fonck's request before his family who in December 1909 gave Pius X five million francs which he passed on to Fonck for the purchase of a house.

Monsignor Thomas Kennedy, rector of the North American College from 1901 to 1917, brought Fonck's attention to a palazzo in the square, number 35, which was about to come onto the market. Fonck immediately acquired the building, the work of the architect Mattia De Rossi, said to have been Bernini's favorite pupil. It had been erected on the site of a still earlier palazzo, the Rossianum, shown to be near the ruins of a Roman temple of the sun on a plan of the city drawn in 1551 by Leonardo Bufalini. The four columns to the main entrance, now blocked off to form a library, are thought to have come from the old temple. In a room at the southern end of the palazzo there were frescoes first thought to be by Nicholas Poussin (he died in Rome in 1665) and Claude Lorrain but later believed to belong to the school of Botticelli. Further financial help required for the adaptation of the building came from Theodore Kohn, the retired Archbishop of Olmütz, and William O'Connell of Boston. The work of adaptation was begun early in 1911 and the building formally opened on February 25, 1912. Seventeen years later a site on the north of the same square was cleared to make way for the new Gregorian University building.

In 1913 Pius X, as a gesture of his continuing interest, loaned the institute for a period the Rocca di Subiaco as a holiday house for professors and students. It was little used during the war and later became the seminary of the diocese of Subiaco. The pope also expressed a wish that the institute should establish a house in the Holy Land. The first site considered by Fonck was on Mount Carmel. When this proved impracticable the pope in 1913 suggested that Fonck should look for a place in Jerusalem. Indefatigable as always, he found and acquired a site in the east of the city not far from the Greek convent. But with the outbreak of war in 1914 and Fonck's departure from Rome the project got no further. Other professors were also forced to leave Italy, some were conscripted and consequently, as with the Gregorian, the number of students fell off. However, with the return of peace Benedict XV in his encyclical *Spiritus Paraclitus* of June 20, 1920 found occasion to praise the work done by the institute in its first ten years and again urged the foundation of a house in the Holy Land.

With changed conditions in Palestine after the war, Fonck's site had to be abandoned. Benedict XV gave his blessing to another chosen near the Joppa gate. The foundation stone was laid after his death and the building opened in 1927. It had been Benedict's expressed wish that the Jerusalem house should devote itself to archeological and geographical research so as not to compete with the long established work of the Dominican Fathers. But post-war disturbances in Palestine made it impossible to carry out this directive. Instead the house was first used by students who had completed their studies in Rome and then by other groups who came for formal courses with their own professors; others joined them in the summer for excursions to Syria, Egypt and Palestine. An account of one journey reads like this: "Ten men, almost all students of the institute, traveled through Palestine at the very end of August. In September they went to Syria. In the beginning of October they visited the northern parts of the Negeb desert, and in the second part of

the month Mount Sinai, going on from there into Egypt as far
as Karnack and Luxor. Two who took part in this journey fell
sick and had to spend some time in a clinic in Jerusalem. Hap-
pily neither was in grave danger." At other times the house became the base for special excursions organized for preachers,
mainly in the months of April and May.

In 1918 before the foundation of the Jerusalem house, the
Biblical Institute planned its first excavations. A site was chosen
on the island of Elephantine in upper Egypt. The finds were divided between the museum in Cairo and the newly founded museum of the institute. In 1929 the first excavations were started
in biblical country. Fr. Alexander Mallon, the superior of the Jerusalem house, picked on a site in Transjordan not far from
where the river falls into the Dead Sea. It was named Telelāt
Ghassūl. Excavations eventually revealed four or five cities built
successively on the same site until the last of them was destroyed
in a great fire and its ruins left undisturbed for four thousand
years. Much was uncovered, including pottery, the foundation of
houses, tombs with frescoes, and some absolutely unique early
paintings. Two talented Brothers, Vives, a Spaniard, and
Decher, a German, took part in the work, repairing pottery and
taking photographs, but after some years the operation had to
be abandoned because of expense.

It was a time when there was a strong desire among arche-
ologists to seek in excavations confirmation of the biblical stories. The work at Ghassūl was important but not in the way that
Fr. Mallon had hoped; it threw no new light on the period of
Abraham as had first been claimed. Nor had he come upon the
site of Sodom and Gomorrah as he at one time believed, but it
revealed an entire primitive culture hitherto unknown. It was
given the name "ghassuliana" and was later uncovered in a
number of other places in the Holy Land.

The Gregorian University had also benefited from the enlightened interest of Benedict XV in ecclesiastical studies. He
had himself followed the courses there as a student at the Capranica. The creation of a new chair of ascetical and mystical
theology in 1918 was largely due to him. It was a far-sighted
move that took account of the growing interest in ascetical stud-

ies and the new and widespread preoccupation with mysticism. Until then the subjects had received only superficial treatment mainly by writers with little training. It was hoped also that the new chair would help to correct the distortions which Jesuit spiritual writers had suffered at the hands of men ill-informed of its sources, and of others, like Abbot Chapman of Downside Abbey, who set authentic mystical prayer in stark opposition to Ignatian spirituality as he conceived it.* Pope Benedict himself had a further motive in setting up the chair, which he expressed in a letter of November 10, 1919 to Fr. Ottavio Marchetti, its first occupant. He wished it to serve not only students of the university "but also the large number of priests in the city whose task it is to direct the souls of others."

About the same time another chair was founded at the Gregorian to provide higher education in philosophy for both laity and clergy. Under its first director, Fr. Garagnani, it met with immediate success and developed into a faculty for culture and religion, providing courses, attended also by religious Sisters, in philosophy, apologetics, Church history and some specialized subjects. It functions today in changed circumstances as the Institute of Religious Sciences. Furthermore, under Benedict XV, between 1919 and 1922, several other new chairs were established—for biblical and patristic theology, paleography, modern philosophy, the history of religion and other subjects. In a number of these areas help was given by the professors of the newly established Biblical Institute. This was the university's response to the general trend toward specialization in scientific studies of all kinds, and it marked the end of the age of great teachers whose erudition ranged far and wide over fields they now had to leave to specialists. Already, before the end of Benedict's pontificate, the Gregorian was on its way to becoming once more a world center for higher ecclesiastical studies. The same period saw the launching of the first of several periodicals by the

---

*Cf. *The Spiritual Letters of Dom John Chapman*, edited with an introductory memoir by R. Hudleston, O.S.B. (1935), which totally misrepresents Jesuit teaching on prayer as was pointed out in several places by Archbishop Goodier, S.J., with particular reference to the letters in part 3 (nos. 82–95, pp. 191–284) addressed to a Jesuit scholastic.

university, the *Gregorianum*, devoted to theological and philo-sophical research. The first number was produced by the univer-sity press in 1920. The review soon attained distinction by its specialized studies in Thomism.

Within a few years after the first world war the Gregorian University, like the Biblicum, was set to expand in a measure that must have well surpassed the dreams of its optimistic founder in the sixteenth century.

13

Closely connected with the Biblicum in its origin and now associated with the Gregorian University was another enterprise of Benedict XV, which taken by itself is proof enough of the creative vision of a great pontiff. By a Motu Proprio, *Orientis Catholici,* dated October 17, 1917, Benedict set up the Oriental Institute. It was no sudden inspiration. The preparatory work had been begun several years earlier. Its aim was to form an élite among the clergy, experts in the Eastern churches, their rites, history, spirituality, canon law and liturgy, which was then a *terra incognita* in Roman ecclesiastical studies. In a more distant prospect it was to work also toward an understanding with the Orthodox churches which might lead to the union which had been the short lived and elusive achievement of the Council of Florence. The pope's breadth of vision is reflected in the provision of places for students from churches not in visible unity with Rome. Today perspectives have changed but in 1917 the horizon could scarcely have been broader. The pope relied greatly for help from the Benedictines, but the Society of Jesus was asked to find occupants for the chairs of controversy and oriental archeology, and in the next year, a third Father for biblical exegesis.

Formerly, in the Congregation of Propaganda, a special section had concerned itself with the affairs of the Oriental churches united to the Holy See. There existed also a pontifical commission for the reunion of dissident churches which Leo XIII had called together only rarely in his last years. Pius X, whose knowledge of the East was confined to his contacts with the Armenian Mekhitarites in the lagoon of Venice, had shown no interest in Oriental Christians. On one occasion in 1908 he had participated in the celebration of the fifteenth centenary of St. John Chrysostom but, as a French writer put it, *ce ne fut qu'un épisode sans lendemain.* The pontifical commission continued to appear in the *Gerarchia cattolica,* the predecessor of the *Annuario Pontificio,* until 1909, when it was heard of no more. At Pius' shoulder, however, as his Secretary for Briefs, was Monsignor Marini. Often when Marini was received in private audience he spoke about Russia and the East, but the pope would shrug the matter off with some pleasantry. "Well," he said to him on one occasion, "we shall have to nominate you Curé of Petersburg."

Benedict XV shared in many ways the outlook of Leo XIII. From 1883 he had been secretary to Cardinal Rampolla, Leo's Secretary of State, and later was sub-Secretary of State under Cardinal Merry del Val, until 1907 when he was consecrated Archbishop of Bologna, to be nominated a cardinal just three months before the death of his predecessor. To prepare for changes certain to follow the end of the first world war, Benedict, before establishing the Oriental Institute, in a Motu Proprio, *Dei Providentis,* of May 1, 1917, had raised the section of Propaganda dealing with Oriental Christians to the rank of a Congregation. In the following November, Marini was nominated its secretary while the pope reserved to himself the post of Prefect.

Although Benedict XV showed perfect impartiality during the war, he was uneasy about its possible results: he feared a German victory might increase Protestant influence in Europe, and on the other hand, he feared equally that an allied victory would bring about the hegemony of an anti-clerical France and an orthodox Russia barely tolerant of Roman Catholicism. With many others he foresaw clearly the dissolution of the Austro-

Hungarian Empire and the special care that would have to be taken of Oriental Christians in the new nations into which the old empire would split.

Already before the end of the war the need for preparedness was made clear when, after the 1917 revolution in Russia, Georgia proclaimed its independence and considered seeking reunion with Rome. The country had never entered discussions with the Holy See nor made contact with it except in the seventeenth century through the intermediary of some Theatine missionaries. At Constantinople there existed a small Georgian community of Benedictines with the privilege of celebrating the liturgy in the Byzantine-Georgian, Armenian and Latin rites. Before the war there had been four young Georgians in the Greek College. When the reports of Georgia's intentions were confirmed, the newly established Oriental Congregation sent out a Visitor in 1919, Fr. Antoine Delpuch, who took with him as a companion a Melkite priest. They were well received and arrangements were made for a mission to be sent to Georgia consisting of three Jesuits who knew Russian well. By the time the Jesuit party reached Constantinople the Bolsheviks had invaded Georgia. The priests busied themselves in Constantinople with the establishment of a college for Russian emigrés which was later transferred to Namur and eventually to the outskirts of Paris.

Benedict's preparedness for peace took the allies by surprise. In September 1918 the Turks capitulated and Constantinople was occupied by French troops. Benedict at once came forward with a plan which illustrated the broadness of his outlook. While the allies were still disputing whether Turkey should be left a foothold in Europe, Benedict proposed that he himself should take over the great Church of Santa Sophia, converted into a mosque in the fifteenth century, with the intention of handing it back to the Greek orthodox patriarch of the city. "This idea," writes the historian of the Oriental Institute,* "was worthy of his great heart and had it been realized would have had repercussions throughout the whole orthodox world. A pro-

*Cirillo Korokesvskij, *Les Origines de la Congregation Orientale et de l'Institut Oriental,* (ms.) p. 105.

posal was prepared on the subject, probably by the Congregation for Extraordinary Affairs, and was even printed." The author continues: "I have seen it without being given the opportunity to read it but Père Varouchas confided to me some of its contents. . . . And I have no more information on it. But apart from Kyr Denys Varouchas who is still alive (1954) I believe I am the only person who has any recollection of the matter."

Clerics in Rome were almost as ignorant of Eastern Christians as the rest of the Western Catholic world. It was, of course, known that there were priests in the city who celebrated Mass in some strange rite or other. They knew of the existence of the Greek College with its Church of St. Athanasius or of the Armenian seminary next to the Church of St. Nicholas of Tolentino or of the Maronites or the Abbey of St. Nilus at Grottaferrata. But these Eastern Catholics were looked on with curiosity more than with active interest. In addition to ignorance of the East there was gross prejudice propagated often by priests of influence. The attitude is well illustrated in a theological textbook published in the last part of the nineteenth century that had a long vogue in a large number of seminaries. "The Greek church," writes Fr. Christian Pesch,* "once the fertile mother of saints has since the schism produced no saint nor anyone outstanding for his sanctity. If we are to believe the tales commonly in circulation by those who have seen the schismatic clergy, monks and nuns, especially in the kingdom of Russia, the greatest part of them is in a state of very great corruption and ignorance and addicted largely to drunkenness. Anyone wanting to commend the Russian church for its holiness would find very few to give him credence." He continues in the same vein for considerable length, admirably illustrating Benedict's insistence on the need for a proper understanding of Eastern Christians. "Yet it cannot be denied," Pesch admits, "that it is possible to find among heretics and schismatics men who lead a good life according to the light of their faith and devotion." Then he ends with a statement that shows there were still theologians in the West who had not changed their approach to the Orthodox

*Praelectiones Dogmaticae, vol. 1, p. 256 (Freiburg, 1894).

church since the time of the Crusades, "Those whom God wishes to sanctify," he claims, "he will lead into the Catholic Church."

It was with this mentality that the Oriental Congregation had to contend. The reaction of the pope's friend, Fr. Korolevskij, to Christian Pesch was virulent. He points out that drunkenness is a national vice of Catholic Ireland every bit as much as of Orthodox Russia and that there have, in fact, been many monks, priests and laymen canonized in the East either by episcopal authority or popular acclaim as used to happen in the whole Church before "Rome reserved to itself the monopoly of canonization; moreover there have been many martyrs done to death by the Turks because they would not embrace Islam." And in any case, he insisted, most Orthodox faithful know nothing of the schism except that it was a quarrel involving the heads of religion.

Benedict XV went ahead. While Marini was a great enthusiast, anxious to do all he could for Eastern Christians, his knowledge did not match his zeal. His great merit was to allow himself to represent the interests of the institute to the pope. He was always ready to be used as an intermediary by the true founder of the Oriental Institute, Fr. Antoine Delpuch, a White Father, a Frenchman born in the Midi in 1868. Delpuch had studied philosophy in Algiers and theology in Carthage. From 1894 to 1907 he had been professor of moral theology at the Melchite seminary in Jerusalem before being called to Rome as Vice-Procurator of his Congregation. There he had got to know Monsignor Marini whose interest in the East he shared. By intelligence and hard work he achieved great things. Without a university education, without knowledge of the East save Palestine and Syria and speaking neither English nor German, he accomplished with credit the tasks assigned to him by Benedict XV, among them the mission to Georgia and the apostolic visitation of the Mekhitarist Armenians of Venice. Moreover, his priorities were always correct. He realized clearly that the first task was to overcome the almost incredible ignorance of Oriental Christianity in the West. Once this was done, he saw hope of mutual understanding and friendly contacts. To set the institute on the right lines Benedict could hardly have made a better choice. For a long time Delpuch had seen the need for a scientific institute, a kind of academy, where it would be possible to organize the study of Oriental history, law, literature, languages and the development of ideas in different Eastern Christian communities. In a series of memoranda in which he passed on his ideas to Marini for the consideration of the pope, Delpuch made much of the fact that nearly all the Roman Catholic missions to the East were Latinized and gave the impression that it was not possible to be a Catholic without becoming a Latin. He also pointed out that the unity of rites in the Catholic Church was a dream similar to that of a single language and nationality for all people.

These were the ideas that inspired the foundation of the Oriental Institute. The first courses started on December 2, 1918 in the *Hospitium de Convertendis* in the Piazza Scossacavalli close to St. Peter's. Delpuch had been in charge only a year when he was replaced by the Benedictine Abbot of St. Paul's outside-the-Walls, Hildephonse Schuster (later Cardinal Archbishop of Milan), who remained in charge until October 22, 1922.

The first need was for a library. There existed, of course, the great Vatican collection close to the first site of the institute, but its ancient as well as its modern books were neither classified nor catalogued. Propaganda possessed another large collection but it was mixed pell-mell with other publications and was not put into order until much later. With a large donation placed in his hands Delpuch purchased some essential works. A librarian was found in a monk of St. Nilus's Abbey at Grottaferrata, Arsenio Pellegrini. He purchased many books from *Civiltà Cattolica*, but without knowledge of foreign languages he was hardly the man to do more.

In the *Hospitium* there was a large hall. Cardinal Marini, in his belief that with the foundation of the institute non-Catholic Christians of the East would rush to make their submission to Rome, made plans to convert the hall into a fitting room for their reception. He first renamed it the "Hall of the Patriarchs," then commissioned a series of frescoes intended to represent striking episodes in the history of the Eastern church. The work was given to an Italian painter, Conti, who specialized in portraying the likenesses of saints to be hung in front of St. Peter's on the occasion of canonizations. The cardinal provided him with a list of subjects and an ecclesiastical consultant, who was not particularly brilliant either as an antiquarian or an historian. The subjects chosen included the Council of Chalcedon, the school of Edessa, the visit of Pope John I to Constantinople in 525 to crown for the second time the Emperor Justin I, a Legation of Photius to Rome, the monks of St. Maron massacred by the Jacobites, the approbation of the Slav liturgy by Pope Adrian II in 869, an incident from the Council of Florence, the body of St. Josephat Kuntsevitch floating on the waters of the river Divna and Isidore of Kiev.

The work was almost complete when the artist began to look around for a model for Isidore of Kiev. He approached Fr. Korolevskij who was aghast at the archeological anachronisms perpetrated by Conti. Some concerned details, others could not escape the notice of any educated Oriental Christian: the monks of St. Maron, for instance, martyred in 514 were clothed like eighteenth-century Maronites before a distinct Maronite church existed; in the crowning of Justin I the patriarch of Constantinople was given a round tiara which was not used by the patriarchs until after the fall of Byzantium. It was possible to overpaint a number of the errors, but there were additional mistakes in the legends below the pictures. Korolevskij ended his report to Cardinal Marini by indicating subjects that should have been chosen of which there were detailed descriptions. He received no reply nor did the book with the reproduction of the pictures planned for publication ever appear. When the palace was pulled down and reconstructed in the via della Conciliazione the paintings were not salvaged. Monsignor Amleto Cicognani (later Cardinal), an assessor of the Congregation, agreed with Korolevskij *c'è proprio da arrossire.*

It would be wrong to say that the institute prospered in the lifetime of Benedict XV. The body of professors was not homogeneous: four religious Orders, several Congregations, a number of diocesan priests and three laymen formed the teach-

Benedict XV (1854–1922) from a medal struck to commemorate the founding of the Oriental Institute.

Fr. Felix Cappello (1879–1962)

Fr. (later Cardinal) Augustin Bea (1881–1968)

The Gregorian University, 1930

University Hall, 1956

ing body. Inevitably there was friction and the president lacked the authority to establish harmony. Pius XI considered the foundation premature and thought of closing it. Abbot Schuster wanted to retire but with his retirement he saved the institute from extinction: he advised the newly elected pope to entrust it to the Jesuits, who could provide a homogeneous personnel inspired by the same ideals and having behind them university experience in different countries. In addition there was the difficulty of finding a new president without exciting jealousies. In his Brief, *Decessor noster,* addressed to Fr. Ledóchowski, the General of the Jesuits, on September 14, 1922, the pope made no mention of these problems. He handed over the institute to the Society and at the same time arranged for it to move from the Palazzo Scossacavalli to the top floor of the Biblical Institute. Cardinal Marini, who had worked hard with moderate knowledge for the establishment of the institute but had involved himself in all its disputes, was relieved of the charge of the Oriental Congregation and was made protector and visitor of all the Eastern establishments in Rome. *Une élegante mise à la rétraite,* as one writer put it. The promotion carried with it no special duties; as visitor he could do nothing without the formal authorization of Pius XI which the pope had no intention of giving. Marini died in the following year.

In giving the direction of the institute to the Jesuits, Pius XI appointed Fr. Michel d'Herbigny its President. Formerly a professor of the Jesuit house of studies at Enghien, Belgium, d'Herbigny had specialized in Russian questions. It was only shortly before his appointment that he had arrived in Rome to take charge of young Jesuit priests doing higher courses of religious studies. He remained President for eight years and honorary Vice-President for another two. He has justly been considered the second founder of the institute. A complex character, incessantly active and in close contact with Russia, he was the confidant of Pius IX who entrusted him with several missions to that country.

Four years later, when the Biblical Institute required space for expansion, the Oriental moved to its present site, the old monastery of St. Anthony in the Piazza Santa Maria Maggiore.

There on November 15, 1926 it was solemnly opened by d'Herbigny, now a bishop, in the presence of Monsignor Angelo Roncalli, later Pope John XXIII.

In 1924 Pius XI, formerly librarian of the Ambrosian library in Milan, commissioned Monsignor Eugène Tisserant and Fr. Korolevskij to go on a book hunting expedition through the Balkans and the Near East. About the same time the Bolsheviks, then in desperate need of foreign exchange, put on the market several fine collections confiscated from the suppressed monasteries in the Soviet Union. D'Herbigny was quick to snatch them up and have them transported to Rome via Odessa and Leghorn. As he built up his library he also increased his staff, calling for assistance from Fr. Cappello, the canonist of the Gregorian University, and from Fr. Erhle and Fr. Fonck from the Biblical Institute, thus preparing the way for Pius XI's move to associate the two institutes with the Gregorian in a single academic consortium.

14

On September 30, 1928 by a Motu Proprio, *Quod Maxime,* Pius XI associated the Biblical and Oriental Institutes with the Gregorian University. All three were Pontifical Institutions and all three were entrusted to the direction of the Society of Jesus. Their history and antecedents were very different. While the Gregorian had been established to educate clergy to meet the challenge of the reformers and the Biblical Institute to counteract the spread of modernism, the Oriental was founded in time to deal with the changed conditions of Europe after the first world war. The pope's plan in associating all three was to form a single university complex that would cater to every branch of ecclesiastical studies at all levels. The three component bodies were to remain autonomous, but at the same time collaborate officially on a broader basis, share an overall responsibility for their studies, and by closer association help each other to attain the purpose for which each was founded. The united group was to be under the immediate direction of the pope.

Pius XI did not make precise the form this cooperation was to take, but in a short time it followed three distinct directions: further exchanges between the professors; the dovetailing of the syllabuses of the three, making the courses of each complemen-

tary both in general and special subjects; and a concerted programme on the development of libraries and publications.

Structurally the Oriental Institute, the smallest and youngest member of the association, underwent fewer changes in the
next decade or two than either the Gregorian or the Biblicum.
After the second world war the Biblical Institute enlarged its
premises and doubled its capacity for students by occupying a
large part of the former house of the Conventual Friars serving
the Church of the Twelve Apostles; a bridge at the south end of
the piazza formed a link between the old palazzo and the new
section. Last of all, the Gregorian, after a cramped existence in
the Palazzo Borromeo for seventy years, moved into a new university building completed in 1930 across the Piazza della Pilotta from the Biblicum. The foundation stone had been laid at
the end of 1924 and every detail of the plans had been examined
time and again by the Jesuit General, Fr. Ledóchowski, who as
Gregory XIII had done during the construction of the Roman
College, frequently visited the site. When later the Gregorian
acquired the Palazzo Frascara an academic square had been
formed in the very heart of Rome.

The years following the foundation of the Consortium saw
an astonishing increase in the number of faculties. In 1928 the
Gregorian had only three, philosophy, theology and canon law;
the Biblical and Oriental one each. The same Motu Proprio,
Quod Maxime, had raised the faculty of Religious Sciences to the
rank of an institute, later to become an academy; now the chairs
established by Benedict XV for history, missiology, spirituality
and social sciences all in their turn grew into faculties. In 1932
a second faculty of the Ancient Orient was set up at the Biblical
Institute. In 1928 the three members of the Consortium had in
all sixty-five professors, a contingent that swelled in the course
of the next forty years to over three hundred. In 1931 the Constitution *Deus Scientiarum Dominus* which added a number of subjects to the general courses of philosophy and theology could
only be put into effect by cooperation between the three. To the
original Jesuit staff of the institutes were added numerous diocesan priests and religious of other Orders, some religious Sisters
and a number of laymen.

Tiding over the change from the old order to the new was a pupil of Cardinal Billot, a brilliant young member of the faculty of theology, Fr. Maurice de la Taille.* Treating of the Mass he gave the same emphasis that Billot had done to the idea of sacrifice, but at the same time he developed his own distinct thesis, so original and simple that it evoked widespread enthusiasm. In his *Mysterium Fidei,* the work of a lifetime, de la Taille maintained that the Last Supper and Calvary completed each other as oblation (or offering) and immolation (or death of the victim) to form one redemptive sacrifice, and that each Mass was an oblation of the once immolated Christ. Although the thesis of the *Mysterium Fidei* had its opponents, it must be reckoned one of the great works by a professor of the Gregorian in this century: with its width of vision, its skillfully presented arguments and erudition, expressed in clear and elegant Latin, and most of all its fusion of specialist theology with devotion it gave a worldwide stimulus to eucharistic piety in the thirties. Today it is thought to be based on a wrong interpretation of the Epistle to the Hebrews and finds few supporters.

Another link between the old order and the new was Fr. Arthur Vermeersch, the moralist, who taught at the Gregorian from 1918 to 1934. His *Summa* of moral theology and his *De Castitate* were probably the best of his almost continuous literary output. He was an independent thinker with a sometimes eccentric manner of treating his subject from the rostrum. There was never a dull moment in his lectures, illuminated always by stories or by jokes directed to one or other national group in the auditorium. "What is a honeymoon?" he once asked his class. "Ut dicunt Angli," he answered, "a moonshine journey." Yet as one of his students wrote: "Perhaps the best proofs of Vermeersch's influence and effectiveness are that we remember or think we remember every word he said. When confronted with a moral problem we either know Vermeersch's answer or at least

*Unfortunately Cardinal Billot, because of his sympathy with *Action Française,* an extreme monarchist movement in France which drew its support mainly from intellectuals and a large section of the clergy, felt obliged to resign from the Sacred College in 1927, when the movement was condemned by Pius XI, and ended his days at the Jesuit noviceship at Galloro, near Rome in 1931.

we know how the master himself would have set about solving it. In that sense he gave us not merely learning, but a fine theological formation."*

Side by side with Vermeersch, among the best remembered professors, was Fr. Felix Cappello, a worthy successor of Wernz, who taught canon law from 1920 to 1962. If Vermeersch was sought after as a spiritual director, Cappello was revered as a saint throughout Rome. A man with a worldwide reputation he lectured with admirable clarity and an astonishing memory that enabled him to cite canons, decretals, answers of the Rota, without ever referring to his book. He was a consultant of four Roman Congregations and a member of three Curial Commissions, besides holding other posts of importance. In various ways he was used by the Holy See in the preparatory work done for the Second Vatican Council. In writing or in conversation he gave expert advice to countless persons. At regular times he could be seen making his way from the Gregorian to Sant' Ignazio where his confessional was always thronged by penitents of every class of Roman society. With all this activity he produced some classic works on canon law.* He was the equal of any of the great professors of the Roman College in the sixteenth century. No metaphysician or innovator, his teaching was characterized by a liberal rather than a literal interpretation of the law and was always pastorally inclined. He reached down to the spirit that had inspired the law and in this way saw the law, as the Psalmist had done, as a means of drawing nearer to God. There was no member of the constantly increasing community in which he lived who did not regard him as a saint.

Fr. Joseph Filograssi must also be mentioned as a man of the transitional period. He had attended the Gregorian as a student from the Capranica and had joined the Society after completing his course of philosophy. Four years older than Cappello he died in the same year. While Cappello came from Belluno in the north, the home town of Pope John Paul I, with whom he

---

*Venerabile, vol. XV, no. 1.

*Summa Iuris Publici Ecclesiastici (six editions); De Censuris (four editions); three volumes entitled Summa Iuris Canonici (five editions); De Matrimonio (seven editions); and De Iure Sacramentorum in five volumes.

had family connections, Filograssi was from Apulia. Before coming to the Gregorian he had studied Oriental languages in Beirut, taught in the Leonine seminary at Anagni, where he had been Prefect of Studies, and had directed the College of Nobles at Mondragone. He joined the Gregorian in 1928, the year of *Quod Maxime,* as assistant to Garagnani in the Institute of Religious Sciences, to become a professor of theology twelve months later. As a consultor of the Oriental Congregation he was closely associated with the Oriental Institute where he also taught. He was called upon by Pius XII to give his opinion on the definability of the Assumption which he later synthesized in two authoritative articles in the *Gregorianum.** He was a devoted member of the staff but no mere *laudator temporis acti.* He represents a host of professors who made and are making a steady, highly technical, substantial and unsung contribution to the work of the Gregorian.

Fr. Pascal d'Elia was as different as could be from any man so far mentioned. He died the year after Filograssi but his work takes the story back to the days of Clavius and Ricci. He was one of the most eminent sinologists of his time and his assistance to authors is acknowledged in a score of books on ancient China. It could perhaps be said that while Ricci with his scientific knowledge and instruments won his way into the walled city of Peking, d'Elia as a philosopher penetrated deeply to the roots and origins of Chinese religious thought. Without engaging in controversy he sought to trace the evolution of the idea of a supreme being from the very ancient texts of Chinese thinkers down to modern times. He collected and edited philological papers in innumerable articles which formed a unique corpus of significant research. From 1940 to 1945 he was Dean of the Faculty of Missiology at the Gregorian and conducted at the same time classes in Chinese languages and literature at the University of Rome. But he was also concerned with the China of his own day and with the establishment of a Chinese Catholic hierarchy. He is a man who merits a memoir to himself.

---

*Gregorianum, vol. 29 (1948) and vol. 31: "Traditio divino-apostolica et assumptio B.V.M."

Engelbert Kirschbaum belonged to the same generation as d'Elia. From 1939 he taught archeology, one of the subjects introduced by the Constitution *Deus Scientiarum Dominus*, both at the Gregorian and at the Institute of Christian Archeology. Between 1941 and 1947, along with Fr. Antonio Ferrua, he took a leading part in the excavations under the "Confession" of St. Peter's in search for the tomb of the Prince of the Apostles. Among his many writings *The Roman Catacombs and Their Martyrs* remains a classic.

With other Gregorian professors who were engaged in the preparatory work for the Second Vatican Council were Frs. Sebastian Tromp and Edouard Dhanis. Their presentation of the first schema on Revelation suffered that same fate as Franzelin's in the First Vatican Council. It was rejected by the assembled Fathers. Both were old men, traditionalists regarded pejoratively as "Roman" theologians. A new draft was prepared by non-Romans, to which Fr. Phillips of Louvain, a former student of the Gregorian, made the main contribution, along with Cardinal Bea, a former professor there. The incident underlined the gap between the old and the young which it has been the task of more recent rectors of the university to bridge.

In the case of Fr. Charles Boyer, still to be seen sitting behind a typewriter at the age of ninety-six, an exception must be made to the rule of not mentioning the living.* A specialist in St. Augustine, a professor of theology, and for many years in charge of studies, his work attained equal distinction in different areas. At the request of the French hierarchy he wrote a complete manual of philosophy for the use of French seminaries. With his close friend, Giovanni Battista Montini, then pro-Secretary of State, he founded in Rome the Centro Unitas before the word ecumenism came into common currency.* With the center went a review of the same name published in French, Italian and English. As a Jesuit he received a unique honor when

---

*This was written in August 1979. Fr. Boyer died on Feb. 23, 1980.

*An indication of his closeness to Montini is his forecast at the time of the conclave in 1963 that should his friend be elected pope he would choose the name of Paul, the first of that name since 1605.

he was appointed not merely a lecturer but the Secretary of the Academia di San Tommaso. In the course of his brief pontificate of thirty-three days, Pope John Paul I, whose thesis on Rosmini Boyer had directed, sent his former tutor greetings on three separate occasions.

While prefect of studies at the Gregorian it was Boyer's task to carry out the prescriptions contained in the 1931 Constitution *Deus Scientiarum Dominus* which added many subjects to the syllabus of seminaries. This Boyer did with skill. He was aware of the dangers a slavish interpretation of the pope's wishes would cause, but insisted: "It is our law" and, without writing an eulogium of the Constitution, showed how it could lead to a broader ecclesiastical education. Three weeks after the promulgation of the Constitution, Pius XI appointed the cardinal in charge of the Sacred Congregation for Seminaries the Grand Chancellor of the university and its associated institutes. In the same year, two new faculties were set up, for Church history and missiology. It was in Boyer's time also that the North American College began to send its men to the Gregorian.

Before crossing the piazza to the Biblical Institute leave can be taken of the Gregorian at the end of term, June 20, 1947, when the university broke up and made its way to Sant' Ignazio, where in the eighteenth century the students of the English College fought unseemly skirmishes with the Greeks who on occasion occupied their places in the church. "Despite the ancient rule, *plausus vetantur*," writes a witness, "we clapped out all professors, tipped our hats to friend and foe, and shook the Gregorian dust from our slightly moth-eaten *soprane.* The exhortation was given in Sant' Ignazio by Fr. Dezza, the Rector Magnificus. His words were an encouragement to us to follow in the footsteps of a distinguished former student of the Gregorian and, incidentally, one very much in the minds of English Catholics today—Archibishop Stepinac.* Benediction followed at the

---

*Alojzize Cardinal Stepinac, born of Croatian peasant parents in 1898, attended the Gregorian University as a member of the German College in 1924, was ordained in 1930, and appointed Archbishop of Zagreb in 1937. He defended Church rights against both the National Socialists and Communists, opposed

altar of St. Aloysius. The German College sang a motet and then hundreds of clerics dispersed as suddenly as they had come."*

Over the piazza at the Biblicum one encounters the monumental figure of Fr. Augustin Bea, who directed the institute during the years following the foundation of the Consortium. He spent thirty-five years of his life there, nineteen of them as rector. Only during his last nine years did he become an international figure, the best known cardinal outside of Rome. He was the only son of a carpenter in the village of Riedböhrigen in the Black Forest. From 1924 to 1928 he had taught Scripture at the Biblicum while at the same time taking charge of the young Jesuits doing advanced courses in theology. In 1930 he was appointed rector of the Biblicum. He held this office until 1949 but remained on the staff there until he was made a cardinal by Pope John XXIII in 1959. During these years, from 1931–51, he also acted as Editor of the periodical *Biblica* and helped to launch a second review of equal importance, namely *Orientalia*. Among the multiple tasks given him by successive popes (he was, incidentally, confessor to three of them), the new translation of the Psalms which he supervised is most open to criticism, not so much for its accuracy as for the manner in which it drained the book of much of its mystical impact. His work at the Secretariate for Christian Unity does not enter into a history of the Gregorian. Excluding numerous articles and printed lectures on ecumenism in the last period of his life, the bibliography of his writings contains one hundred and sixty-eight items of which one hundred and twenty-six are concerned with the Bible. In his lectures, which were always carefully prepared and set out, he showed himself familiar with every school of exegesis. His discreet though decisive approach to the interpretation of different types of literature in the Bible can be seen in Pius XII's encyclical *Divino Afflante Spiritu* (1943), prepared

---

forced conversion and racial persecution, and assisted thousands of persecuted Jews, Slovenes and Serbs. Arrested in September 1946 he was tried on trumped up charges of collaborating with the Germans during the war and sentenced to sixteen years imprisonment. From 1951 he was kept under house arrest and died in December 1952.

*Venerabile, vol. 13 (1947).

largely by him and the Dominican Fr. Vosté, which formed a landmark in progressive thinking on the Bible. His years as rector saw the foundation of a second faculty, for Oriental Antiquities, in which all the principal languages of the Near East, from Sumerian to Coptic and Armenian, were taught. This also indicated Bea's interest in sciences subsidiary to the Scriptures.

While during these years the Biblical Institute shared its findings more and more with the scholars in Europe and the United States, the Oriental Institute, where Bea also lectured, was seeking in the rich spiritual tradition of the East a new ground for mutual understanding. Fr. Irenaeus Hausherr, who joined its staff in 1927, nursed the study of Eastern spirituality from its infancy, so to speak, to a mature science. In a long series of articles in the publications of the institute he explored the hidden wisdom of the East from the third century to the Middle Ages. In his work, for example, on the meaning of compunction in the Eastern monastic tradition he revealed the liberating, joyful and creative aspects of Christian penance and the importance of communication and companionship between principal and master in spiritual direction. While studying Syriac ascetics of the fourth century he identified a charismatic movement liable to aberrations but also open to the genuine impulses of the Holy Spirit. His work, taken with that of the others at the institute, shows the almost revolutionary change of approach to the Eastern churches by Western Christendom.

A pioneer in a different field of Oriental studies was Fr. Guillaume de Jerphanion. A Frenchman from Pontèves he joined the Jesuits of the Lyons Province and laid the groundwork of his immense knowledge of Christian Cappadocia while teaching as a scholastic at Tokat in Anatolia. After ordination he was able to continue his researches for five months (August 1911 to January 1912) during which he discovered a number of Cappadocian churches and chapels hitherto known only to local peasants. He then began to compile an inventory of Cappadocian monasteries and paintings which he completed at the Russian Institute in Constantinople. After serving as a Turkish-speaking officer in the French forces in the first world war he joined the Oriental Institute as professor of archeology in 1918;

141

his particular field of interest was threefold: the architecture of the basilica, iconography, and liturgical instruments. This last led to a work of unmatched importance on the chalice of Antioch.

But his literary monument is the seven volumes on the churches of Cappadocia (1925–1942). His mastery of the subject is seen in the clear divisions and subdivisions of the chapters, his choice of illustrations and his description of churches and particularly his analysis of the paintings.

It can be claimed that he achieved something beyond the immediate purpose of the work, for he showed that the Syro-Palestinian Christian art had not entirely disappeared in the iconoclastic upheavals of the fifth and sixth centuries, but had survived especially in Cappadocia. His illustrations presented an art-form more simple, provincial, spontaneous and moving than the classic imperial art of Constantinople. Fr. de Jerphanion also made it clear that the Cappadocian painting had influenced not only the Byzantine renaissance but Western art as well and, in particular, Western iconography. Fr. de Jerphanion lectured within weeks of his death in October 1948. He is remembered as a priest of great charm and quiet habits of work.

In 1936, five years after the establishment of the Consortium, the Oriental Institute divided its periodical, *Orientalia Christiana*, into two, the first section, *Analecta*, dealing with monographs, the second, *Periodica*, with more domestic concerns of the institute. At the same time a project was launched that today has greater significance than its founders could have envisaged. The title chosen for it was *Concilium Florentinum: Documenta et Scriptores.*

At Florence on July 6, 1439 Greeks and Latins had sealed and proclaimed the union of their churches after nearly two years of preparatory discussions. Among the Greeks present had been the Patriarch of Constantinople with twenty Oriental metropolitans, some of them also officially representing the patriarchs of Alexandria, Antioch and Jerusalem. Later the union was rejected by the Greek Church on the ground that it had been reached under coercion. Editions of various documents had been published in the seventeenth century but the institute, under the direction of Fr. Georg Hofmann, set about providing new critical editions of all the documents, published and unpublished, concerning the council—letters, diaries, decrees, speeches, everything including the *Journey of the Metropolitan Isidore to the Council,* describing the routes followed by the Russian delegation. Isidore first went to Moscow. When he reached Riga he was refused permission to cross Lithuanian territory and had to wait three months for the Baltic ice to break up before continuing his journey by sea to Lübeck. On arriving in Italy he and his party were amazed at all they saw—the stone houses, the bridges, the fine buildings and vineyards. This is a fascinating volume in the series, the first of which appeared in 1940 and the last in 1976, a timely and vital work of the institute when today, after five centuries, preparations are being made for the renewal of discussions between East and West.

When Fr. Aemilius Herman died in January 1963 he had been professor of Oriental canon law at the institute for almost thirty years. His articles, gathered into four volumes, covered every aspect of the subject but especially marriage and the sacraments and had prepared the way for the erection of a faculty of Oriental canon law in 1971. Other works of the institute, such as the preparation of a critical edition of Syriac anaphoras, are too technical to be more than mentioned in a book of this kind. A recent initiative has been launched in the realm of Christian Arab literature. It would doubtless have surprised Christian Pesch to learn that ten percent of the Arab-speaking world is Christian, and that some thousand books are published every year in Arabic on Christian Arabic theology. In the West no faculty or chair deals with the subject. It is taught only at the Oriental Institute where a beginning has been made also with a small review and the publication of texts with notes and introductions.*

By sharing the contacts which each member of the Consor-

---

*The first volume edited by Samir Khalil, *The Lamp of Understanding,* a kind of general catechism by a Copt of the thirteenth century, opens a series which owes much to the generosity of the Melchite Bishop of Aleppo; another four volumes are in preparation.

tium made with scholars all over the world, they increasingly benefited each other as the ancient suspicions between Catholic and Protestant, East and West, gave place to mutual appreciation. In all three, scientists and theologians receive an equally warm welcome as was given Galileo on his first visit to the Roman College in 1611. Members of the Eastern Churches found a second home in the Oriental Institute. An entry like this in its journal for 1937 can be multiplied several times: "The Patriarch of the Maronites, Peter Arida, with his attendants, which included two bishops, were entertained by the Institute." In the Biblicum and Gregorian eminent scholars from Europe and the United States made their way to the professors' rooms without bothering first to see that their horses were saddled and ready in the event of their having to make a quick getaway.

Every year the Biblical and Oriental Institutes added names to their roll of distinguished alumni. For instance, in December 1958, Paul Cheikho, Bishop of Aleppo, who had studied at the institute from 1930–1933, was elected Patriarch of the Chaldeans, and in 1968 another alumnus of the institute, Ignatius Antony Hayek, became the Syro-Catholic Patriarch of Antioch. In 1963 Fr. Athanasius Wlykyi, O.S.B.M., was appointed Superior General and Proto-Archimandrite of his Order. Bishops apart, the Biblicum can claim fourteen cardinals, including Frings, Lercaro and Liénart, as its former students. But its greatest work has been to provide the Church with some four thousand exegetes who through their teaching in seminaries and university faculties have helped Christians of all denominations to a better understanding and appreciation of the Holy Scriptures.

Epilogue

The aim of St. Ignatius in founding the Roman College in 1551 was pastoral and missionary. He saw it as a training ground for priests, bishops, missionaries and laymen whose education would match the best in his day and would march *pari passu* with attachment to the Holy See. Basically the aim of his foundation has not changed. Communication has replaced controversy, but both Bellarmine and Bea must be equally honored. The Roman College, now the Gregorian University, while revering its host of heroes and martyrs, sees its mission today in terms of revealing Christ to all humankind stretching out, knowingly or not, toward God, from Ricci's China to de Nobili's India, a mission best fulfilled by three foundations working together as a single unit. Side by side with Italians, Greeks, Germans, English and Armenians are men from countries undiscovered or undeveloped in the sixteenth century. When Gregory XIII was thanked in twenty-five languages for his great benefaction even he could scarcely have forseeen that four hundred years later his university of the nations would be attended by students from eighty-five or more countries and have professors from a continent then unknown even to the men who held the chair of Clavius. If a university leaves a stamp on a man, as it should, then the Conventual Franciscan Maximilian Kolbe at Auschwitz can easily link hands across the centuries with Rudolf Acquaviva at Akbar's court.

Jerome Nadal, the most faithful interpreter of Ignatius' mind, spoke to the first students of the Roman College in terms that anticipated Vatican II. "Christ is the infinite Word of God," he said. "We are ministers of that Word. We cannot explain the grandeur of that ministry but only feel its effects."

The *Liber Annualis* of the Gregorian records frequent invitations which professors answer every year to lecture at conferences in other universities: Tokyo, Oxford, Madrid, Toronto, New York and Berkeley, occur most frequently in the lists. But unrecorded is the help, usually confidential, given by some fifty-five professors to different curial congregations, commissions and other bodies, whether for the reform of canon law, the production of an Italian adult catechism, or for the preparation of the agenda for an episcopal synod. The list is a long one. To mention only the Institute of Spirituality, there are few of its staff not engaged in assisting Religious Congregations of men and women in revising their constitutions to meet present day needs.

Certainly, the university is alive. The recently founded center for Marxist studies possesses a library perhaps unique of its kind anywhere: the reader can find in it works published in Russia which one after another have been withdrawn from the shelves of libraries in the Soviet Union. The director accompanied Cardinal König to Yugoslavia in 1974 to see whether a "dialogue" could be started there between Catholics and Marxists. Quietly the Biblical Institute is working on a new approach to exegesis, relating it more to the needs of the Church and to questions concerning dogma, the priesthood and prayer. While the Gregorian University has rightly waived Latin as a condition for entry, the Biblical Institute demands an entire preliminary year devoted to Hebrew and Greek for those who enter without sufficient knowledge of these languages.

It may be another ten years before it is possible to evaluate the work done in this member of the Consortium. Through historical and philological research it is seeking to penetrate more deeply into the message of the Scriptures. Already it is widely known for its literary analysis of the biblical texts and its study of Ugaritic, a Semitic language discovered only in 1929 and spoken in Palestine when the Israelites first occupied the country. One must resist the temptation at this point to mention names of scholars highly rated in their specialist fields. In addition the institute has given an impetus to the study of the use of Scripture in the Fathers which must surely receive Galileo's benediction from heaven.

Tasks like these can no longer be handled by an exclusively Jesuit staff even though it is drawn from more than eighty provinces of the Society. At present some twenty-one Religious Orders and Congregations both of men and women, as well as some laymen, reinforce the Jesuit effort with great dedication. Ignatius was never a man to believe that he was legislating for all time. He would have abundantly endorsed this development. Today, thanks to contacts made by individual members of the staff, leading professors from Louvain, Chicago, Freiburg, London, Lyons and New Orleans are invited not just to give single lectures but to teach for an entire semester. The result is a full and varied curriculum, attuned to the needs of the time, unlike that of the Roman College in the eighteenth century. Dedication to work that is likely to show results only in a remote future is hard to come by in an age that looks for quick returns for its expenditure of effort. It might be said that the need for such devotion is greatest in the youngest member of the Consortium, namely, the Oriental Institute, where new members of the teaching staff are needed, both young and seasoned professors, from ecumenical theologians to specialists in Georgian and Armenian studies.

To say that the Gregorian group has no growing pains would be an understatement; it has had and is still having expansionist spasms. In 1945 its three members offered a hundred and thirty-three different courses; twenty-five years later the number had multiplied three times. It was the same with seminars. The specialization has meant an increase in staff which in turn has made possible a number of research projects into questions such as the stability of vocations to the priesthood or the types of religious practices in different Italian dioceses. More men has also meant many more publications and the provision of updating courses for shorter or longer periods in subjects like canon law. But although the number of students increases each year the scarcity of vocations and the emphasis placed by Vatican II on national churches account for a smaller enrollment today than twenty years ago.

An institution that remains sensitive to every current and shift of thought in the Church in order to sift and assess the good in it lays itself wide open to criticism from outside. There is criticism also from within, but now the voices of students can at least be heard in a way that was impossible when the tortured young Bellarmine attended the lectures on the *De Anima* of Aristotle in his student days at the Roman College. As long as communications remain open solutions can be only a matter of time.

The expansion has also added to the anxiety of maintenance which St. Ignatius handed on to his professors. "Expenses of the Institute these years have exceeded the revenues. The deficit was made up by the Society." That was written in 1930 by a scribe of the Oriental Institute. Today the deficit of all three members of the Consortium is incalculably greater. But along with the financial burden Fr. Pedro Arrupe has also inherited Ignatius' optimism. Had Polanco been an author and not a secretary he might have written a book instead of a flurry of letters to make the Roman College and its needs known to those who could have helped to make it the model Ignatius wished it to become.

However, in a recent address at the Gregorian Cardinal Garrone, the Grand Chancellor of the university, set everything in its correct perspective. "I knew the Gregorian once a long time ago as a student. And in the last thirteen years I have been the witness and the confidant of the difficulties touching its life and development. Without doubt the material problems are not the most important and more frequently I have had to deal with questions of doctrine than of finance. However, I am aware of the problems arising from the growing number of students and from the disproportion between its precarious resources and the insistent demands made on them. But above all it is the spirit of the university that should be our daily concern. In the troubled milieu of our time it is impossible for a university to avoid difficult problems created by persons or current ideas. But I have never found the Gregorian incapable of facing up to them in a spirit of total loyalty to the Church."

Bibliography

It seems necessary to give an indication of the sources used in this book. Apart from Fr. Riccardo Villoslada's *Storia del Collegio Romano dal suo inizio (1551) alla soppressione della Compagnia di Gesù (1773)*, Rome, 1954, an indispensable work of reference for the early chapters, I have consulted the following:

Unprinted sources
The *Annual Letters* of the Gregorian University, the Biblical and Oriental Institutes; the manuscript of Dr. Oskar Garstein's second volume of his *Rome and the Counter-Reformation in Scandinavia;* the unpublished *Vita del R. P. Lorenzo Ricci* by Tommasso Termanini in the archives of the Roman Province in the Gesù; the typescript of Fr. Korolevskij's *Origines de la Congregation Orientale et de l'Institut Oriental* at the Oriental Institute; and the following items from the archives of the Gregorian University: De Vico's manuscript of his *Elementa Astronomica,* his letter describing his visit to London and the United States in 1848; the Diary of the Roman College; the photographic copy of Newman's summary of his *Essay on Development* and Perrone's comments on it.

UNIVERSITY OF NATIONS

Books

Anon, *The Scots College in Rome*, London, 1930

Bangert, William V., S.J., *A History of the Society of Jesus*, St. Louis, 1972

Brodrick, James, S.J., *Galileo, the Man, His Work, His Misfortunes*, London, 1964
St. Peter Canisius, London, 1935
The Progress of the Jesuits, London, 1946
Blessed Cardinal Bellarmine, vol. 1, London, 1927

Chandlery, P. J., S.J., *Pilgrim Walks in Rome*, London, 1903

Culley, T., S.J., *The Influence of the German College on Music in German-speaking Countries in the Sixteenth and Seventeenth Centuries*, Cologne, 1969

D'Elia, Pasquale M., S.J., *Galileo in China*, Harvard, 1960

Fülöp-Müller, R., *The Power and Secret of the Jesuits*, London, 1957

De Guibert, J., S.J., *La Spiritualité de la Compagnie de Jésus*, Rome, 1953

Hales, E. E. Y., *The Catholic Church in the Modern World*, London, 1958

Langford, Jerome J., *Galileo, Science and the Church*, New York, 1966

Leeming, Bernard I., *Agostino Cardinal Bea*, Notre Dame, 1964

Ligthart, C. J., S.J., *The Return of the Jesuits*, London, 1978

Lukács, Ladislaus, S.J., *Monumenta Paedagogica S.J. (1540–1556)*, 2nd edition, vol. 1, Rome (Instit. Hist. S.J.), 1965

Munday, Anthony, *The English Romayne Life, 1582*, ed. London, 1925

Newman, John Henry, *Letters*, vols. XI and XII, London 1961 and 1962

Micolau, Michael, S.J., *P. Hieronymi Nadal Orationis Observationes*, Rome (Instit. Hist.), 1964

Pastor, L., *History of the Popes*, London

Perrone, Giovanni, S.J., *Praelectiones Theologicae*, (ed. 1845) Rome

Pirri, P., S.J., *L'Università Gregoriana del Collegio Romano nel primo seculo dalla restituzione*, Rome, 1930

Severin, Timothy, *The Oriental Adventure*, London, 1976

Stein, G., S.J., *Specola Vaticana*, Rome, 1952
White, Lancelot Law (ed.), *Roger Joseph Boscovitch*, London, 1961
Wiseman, N., *Recollections of the Last Four Popes*, London, 1858

Periodicals
Acta Pontificii Instituti Biblici (Rome)
    "In Memoriam S.R.E. Card. Augustinus Bea, S.J. (1881–1968)," vol. 7 (no. 5, 1970)

Archivum Historicum Soc. Jesu (Rome)
    "La Tipografia del Collegio Romano," by Giuseppe Castellani, S.J. (no. 2, 1933)
    "Para la historia de la oración en el colegio romano durante la segunda mitad del siglo XVI," by Ignacio Iparraguirre, S.J. (no. 15, 1946)
    "The Correspondence of Father Christopher Clavius preserved in the Archives of the Pont. Gregorian University," by Edward C. Phillips, S.J. (no. 8, 1939)
    "Algunos documentos sobre la música en el antiguo seminario Romano," by Ricardo G. Villoslada, S.J. (no. 31, 1962)

Bulletin of the American Association of Jesuit Scientists (Boston)
    "The Proposals of Father Christopher Clavius, S.J. for improving the teaching of Mathematics," by Edward C. Phillips, S.J. (vol. 18, No. 4)

Gregorianum (Rome)
    "Il B. Olivero Plunket nel Collegio Romano e nel Collegio di Propaganda," by F. G. (vol. 1, 1920)
    "Réflexions sur la Constitution *Deus Scientiarum Dominus*," by C. Boyer, S.J. (vol. 17, 1936)
    "El P. Filippo Febei, S. J. y la fundación de la cátedra de historia ecclesiastica (1741)," by P. de Leturia, S. J. (vol. 30, 1949)

Investigationes Theologico-Canonicae (Rome)
    "Francis Xavier Wernz, S.J.: the last of the Decretalists," by Clarence Gallagher, S.J. (1978)

Jesuit Educational Quarterly
"Jesuit Education and the Jesuit Theatre," by Victor R. Yanitelli (January 1949)

The Month (London)
"Francesco Lana, S.J., Pioneer of Aeronautics (1631–1687)," by Conor Reilly, S.J. (March 1958)

La Nouvelle Revue des Deux Mondes
"L'Institut Biblique de Rome," by Eduard des Places, S.J. (October 1975)

Orientalia Christiana Periodica (Rome)
"La Fondation de l'Institut Pontifical Oriental," by A. Raes (1967, fasc.1)
"Pour les cinquantes premières années de l'Institut Pontifical Oriental," by A. Raes (1967, fasc. 2)
"Early Printed Slavonic Books in the Library of the Oriental Institute," by I. Krajcar, S.J. (1968, fasc.1)
"Concilium Florentinum: Documenta et Scriptores: An ambitious scheme accomplished," by J. Gill, S.J. (1977, fasc. 1)

Oxford Companion to the Theatre (Oxford, 1951)
"Jesuit Drama," by E(dna) P(urdie)

Periodica de Re Morali, Canonica, Liturgica (Rome)
"Cenni storici sulla Facoltà di Dritto Canonico," by Clarence Gallagher, S.J., (vol. 66, 1977)

Studies (Dublin)
"Suarez and Democracy," by Alfred Rahilly (Spring 1918)
"Father Athanasius Kircher, S.J.," by Conor Reilly (Winter 1955)
"Jesuit Men of Science," by Daniel O'Connell, S.J. (Autumn 1956)
"Roger Joseph Boscovitch, Priest and Scientist," by Daniel O'Connell, S.J. (Winter 1962)

Theological Studies
"A Recent Roman Scriptural Controversy," by Joseph A. Fitzmyer, S.J. (vol. 23, 1961)

The Venerabile
  "The Later 'Eighties'," by Ambrose Moriarty, Bishop of
  Shrewsbury (May 1945)
  "Father Vermeersch," by William Butterfield (November
  1950)
  "College Diary," *Passim*

Appendix

Alumni of the Gregorian University:

Saints

Aloysius Gonzaga, S. J., 1568–1591
Camillus de Lellis, M. I., 1550–1614
John Berchmans, S. J., 1599–1621
Robert Bellarmine, S. J., 1542–1621
Leonard of Port Maurice, O. F. M. Cap., 1676–1751
John Baptist De Rossi, 1689–1764
Gaspar Del Bufalo, C.PP.S., 1786–1837
Vincent Pallotti, S. A. C., 1795–1850
Ralph Sherwin, 1550–1581
Luke Kirby, 1548–1582
Polydore Plasden, 1563–1591
Eustace White, 1560–1591
Robert Southwell, S. J., 1561–1595
Henry Walpole, S. J., 1559–1595
John Almond, 1577–1612
Henry Morse, S. J., 1595–1645
John Wall, O. F. M. 1620–1679

David Lewis, S. J., 1617–1679
Oliver Plunket, Archbishop of Armagh, 1629–1681

Blessed

Rudolph Acquaviva, S. J., 1550–1583
Peter Berno, S. J., 1552–1583
Mark Crisino, 1588–1619
Charles Spinola, S. J., 1564–1622
Peter Paul Navarro, S. J., 1560–1622
John Shert, . . .–1582
Robert Johnson, 1544–1582
William Hart, 1557–1583
Thomas Hemerford, 1554–1584
John Munden, 1543–1584
Robert Morton, 1547–1588
Richard Leigh, 1561–1588
Christopher Buxton, 1562–1588
Edward James, 1559–1588
Christopher Bayles, 1564–1590
John Ingram, 1565–1594
Robert Watkinson, 1579–1602
Edward Oldcorne, S. J., 1561–1606
Richard Newport, 1572–1612
John Lockwood, 1561–1642
Antony Turner, S. J., 1628–1679
Anthony Baldinucci, S. J., 1665–1717
Alberic Crescitelli, P.I.M.E., 1863–1900
Maximilian Kolbe, O.F.M. Conv., 1894–1941

Popes

Gregory XV (Alessandro Ludovisi), 1621–1623
Urban VIII (Maffeo Barberini), 1623–1644
Innocent X (Giovanni Battista Pamphilj), 1644–1655
Clement IX (Giulio Rospigliosi), 1667–1669
Clement X (Emilio Altieri), 1670–1676
Innocent XII (Antonio Pignatelli), 1691–1700
Clement XI (Giovanni Francesco Albani), 1700–1721
Innocent XIII (Michelangelo dei Conti), 1721–1724

UNIVERSITY OF NATIONS

Clement XII (Lorenzo Corsini), 1730–1740
Pius IX (Giovanni Mastai-Ferretti), 1846–1878
Leo XIII, (Gioacchino Pecci), 1878–1903
Benedict XV (Giacomo della Chiesa), 1914–1922
Pius XI (Achille Ratti), 1922–1939
Pius XII (Eugenio Pacelli), 1939–1958
Paul VI (Giovanni Battista Montini), 1963–1978
John Paul I (Albino Luciani), 1978